Emory, Washington Co.,
Virginia
Oct. 2015

Museums and Civic Dialogue

Museums and Civic Dialogue

::: **CASE STUDIES FROM ANIMATING DEMOCRACY**

Editors
Pam Korza and
Barbara Schaffer Bacon

AMERICANS *for the* ARTS
WASHINGTON, DC

Americans for the Arts, Washington, DC 20005
 Published 2005
13 12 11 10 09 08 07 06 05 1 2 3 4 5

The photograph on the cover is of Gallery 602, The Andy Warhol Museum, used as a study and dialogue area for the exhibition, *Without Sanctuary: Lynching Photography in America.* September 2001–January 2002. Photo by Richard Stoner.

Book design by studio e_2.

Library of Congress Cataloging-in-Publication Data
Museums and civic dialogue : case studies from Animating Democracy / editors, Pam Korza and Barbara Schaffer Bacon.— 1st ed.
p. cm.
ISBN-13: 978-1-879903-37-1 (alk. paper)
1. Art museums and community—United States. 2. Art museums—Social aspects—United States. 3. Art museums—Educational aspects—United States. 4. Art museums—Exhibitions—Case studies. I. Korza, Pam. II. Bacon, Barbara Schaffer. III. Americans for the Arts (Organization) IV. Animating Democracy (Initiative)
N510.M87 2005
708—dc22
2005020898

ISBN–13: 978-1-879903-37-1
ISBN–10: 1-879903-37-7

The paper used in this publication meets the minimum requirements of the American National Standard for Information Sciences—Permanence of Paper for Printed Library Materials, ANSI Z39.48-1992.

Additional copies available at www.AmericansForTheArts.org/bookstore

Museums and Civic Dialogue: Case Studies from Animating Democracy
is a publication of Animating Democracy.

Animating Democracy, supported by the Ford Foundation,
is a program of Americans for the Arts.

Table of Contents

Preface

MUSEUMS AND CIVIC DIALOGUE features exhibition projects that demonstrate how three museums have functioned as provocative and effective forums for civic dialogue. Focusing on contemporary and conceptual works of art, in the case of Henry Art Gallery and The Jewish Museum, and historic images, in the case of The Andy Warhol Museum, their endeavors highlight new and adapted approaches to curatorial practice, interpretation, and education prompted by civic intention. The case studies also offer insights regarding institutional challenges and changes in practice that necessarily occurred.

From 2000 to 2004, with support from the Ford Foundation, Animating Democracy—an ambitious initiative of Americans for the Arts—provided cultural organizations leading these and other such experiments in arts and humanities-based civic dialogue with funding, opportunities for peer exchange, and other technical support. Animating Democracy set out to demonstrate that civic dialogue and art can be mutually enhanced when the two are thoughtfully brought together. With focus and intention, artists and cultural organization leaders can use the inherent power of art and the humanities to stimulate civic dialogue and engagement.

The cultural organization leaders, artists, dialogue practitioners, and community partners involved in these projects were encouraged to reflect openly and critically about their efforts. In the spirit of experimentation and learning that could be shared with the field, what *didn't* work was welcomed as much as what did. As a result, the case studies provide portraits and practical analyses of the projects that are candid in revealing challenges as well as successes. They detail civic issues addressed, arts and humanities components, and artistic and dialogue methodologies. Whether written by project organizers themselves or by "project liaisons" who shadowed each project, asking questions and helping to draw out what artists, cultural organizers, and partners were experiencing, the case studies reflect a diversity of voices from within the projects and varied styles of presentation.

Featured in *Museums and Civic Dialogue* are:

Gene(sis): Contemporary Art Explores Human Genomics. Through *Gene(sis)*, Henry Art Gallery employed the power of art to provoke dialogue about new developments in the science of human genomics. The case study chronicles an expansive cross-disciplinary series of public programs, through which the Henry raised awareness of economic, moral, and ethical dimensions of the issue and sparked discussion within the gallery and throughout Seattle.

Mirroring Evil: Nazi Imagery/Recent Art. The Jewish Museum's exhibition featured images incorporating Nazi perpetrators as a springboard for dialogue about complicity and complacency toward evil in today's society. The case study examines what happened when the museum ventured into "taboo" subject matter and the use of provocative artwork to reframe the subject of the Holocaust. It analyzes the public reception and intense controversy prompted by the media before the exhibition opened and reflects on the media's effects on public discourse.

The Without Sanctuary Project. The Andy Warhol Museum's project engaged regional audiences in dialogue about race and bigotry through an extensive project centered around 19th- and 20th-century photos and postcards illustrating lynching in the United States. In addition to detailing the many and varied dialogue opportunities and programs developed to help visitors in their exchange on this emotional exhibition, the essay explores the idea of "museum as artist" and provides insight into the tensions and challenges of a largely white institution carrying out this project.

Ron Chew introduces these case studies from his vantage point as executive director of the Wing Luke Asian Museum in Seattle. He looks first internally at Wing Luke's own shift to a dialogue driven and civic engagement approach to exhibitions and programming, catalyzed by its pivotal exhibition, *Executive Order 9066: 50 Years Before and 50 Years After,* about the forced internment of Japanese Americans. Chew then broadens the lens by observing changes in the museum field as institutions seek greater relevance as "community response agents" and "active town halls."

Animating Democracy set out with a serious goal to document the philosophical, aesthetic, and practical dimensions of this work for the benefit of the field and participating artists and organizations. *Museums and Civic Dialogue* is one of five case study volumes in Animating Democracy's Art & Civic Engagement series. These and three other Animating Democracy publications are listed in the back of this book. Together, they offer a deep and holistic look at the work of arts- and humanities-based civic dialogue from many perspectives. They offer new as well as affirmed knowledge drawn from rich practical experience. We hope they will prove to be timely resources, as well as enduring ones, that inform continued vital work in civically engaged art in communities across the United States.

Acknowledgments

WE EXTEND OUR GRATITUDE to the many Animating Democracy participants whose work is the basis for these case studies. It has been a privilege to support and learn from the artists, cultural organization leaders, and community and dialogue partners who made these arts-based civic dialogue endeavors possible. With intelligence and candor they have shared insights and learning in deep and generous ways, demonstrating their commitment to the educational value of the work as well as its impact in their own communities. The artistic and programmatic innovations that have resulted from their arts-based civic dialogue projects have been rewarding to support and experience.

The crafting of these case studies and essays was no small task, involving description of complex multistage and multilayered projects and the representation of the many voices within them. We sincerely thank the writers for their pieces: Jessica Gogan for her deep and expansive thinking about museums "as artists;" Jeanne Pearlman for her keen reflections on The Jewish Museum's aesthetic investigation and the contextual understanding she brings to bear on the media controversy that became such a part of the *Mirroring Evil* story; and Lynn Stern for capturing the scope of Henry Art Gallery's programmatic efforts and the excitement of its approach to merging artistic and scientific inquiry to stimulate civic dialogue. We are sure they will become valued references, teaching tools, and resources that will contribute to field discourse for some time to come.

For his thoughtful introduction, we thank Ron Chew whose peer perspective lends field context to as well as on-the-ground appreciation of the work of these museums.

We value the editorial contributions of a great team of editors. John Fiscella and Gayle Stamler's skillful and intelligent content editing have served to draw out important ideas and sharpen the material in valuable ways. We are grateful to Kirsten Hilgeford and Susan Gillespie, editors with Americans for the Arts, for their expert proofreading, additional editorial work, and for overseeing the production process. We thank Anne Canzonetti for her proofreading and editorial contribution on the Art & Civic Engagement series. Our special thanks are extended to studio e_2 for book design that captures so beautifully and functionally the intent and spirit of the publication. The creativity, professional expertise, and hard work of each one have paid off in a resource for the field of which we are very proud.

Thanks to all our colleagues at Americans for the Arts who have offered their ideas and support to Animating Democracy's efforts and to this book in particular, and to the Ford Foundation, without whose vision and support Animating Democracy would not have been possible.

Barbara Schaffer Bacon and Pam Korza
Co-directors, Animating Democracy

Introduction

THOSE OF US WHO HAVE ATTEMPTED to transform the museum from an inward-looking citadel into an active town hall grapple with some significant challenges. How can arts and culture help us confront frontline social issues like racial inequality, poverty, war, and environmental justice? And how can we make viewing and experiencing the "stuff" in the gallery compelling enough that visitors are motivated to see the world in new and profound ways?

In 1992, a year after I was hired as executive director of the Wing Luke Asian Museum, I began working on my very first major project, *Executive Order 9066: 50 Years Before and 50 Years After.* This exhibition opened on the 50th anniversary of the federal order that authorized the forced removal and imprisonment of 110,000 Japanese Americans from the West Coast.

More than 100 Japanese Americans—representing four generations—came together to plan and build this exhibition, in the process documenting untold stories, healing profound emotional wounds in the community, and challenging future generations to think about the complex issue of protecting civil liberties during times of war.

Wing Luke wanted the exhibition, which came simply to be known in verbal shorthand as *9066*, to be a healing agent and a tool for education. Beyond that, though, we wanted to experiment with transforming the museum gallery—traditionally regarded as a passive zone for display of iconic objects—into a live place where the past and the present could be linked through broad and vibrant dialogue. Doing this with *9066*, we knew, would not be easy.

Many surviving internees—who had lost homes, businesses, and their precious freedom during the War—had not, because of the trauma of what happened, shared their personal stories with their own children. Because we wanted the exhibition to speak in the first-person voice of community members and not in the voice of academic scholars, we needed to find ways to attain a level of trust with these individuals, a trust that they had not even granted to their own families. How would we get them to open up and share their stories? How could we make their voices part of our history?

There was profound distrust and animosity between the second-generation Nisei veterans, who had volunteered to fight overseas to prove their loyalty and pave the way for release of their families after the War, and the "No-No Boys," who had gone to prison on principle rather than fight for a country that had abused their constitutional liberties. How could we get both the veterans and the "No-No Boys" to participate together so that we could feature their parallel stories?

Meanwhile, outside the Japanese-American community in the larger public sphere, many individuals still felt the treatment of Japanese Americans was justified. They were vocal and belligerent. Some—motivated, quite simply, by racism—wrote letters in the press and spoke out on radio talk shows, fanning the flames of intolerance, hoping to torpedo the project.

As a newcomer to the museum profession, I sought the advice of several colleagues outside our institution. They were skeptical that we could develop a cohesive display. "You can't create a quality exhibit," I was warned, "if you put the work in the hands of a committee. You'll have too much infighting, too many egos, no artistic control. It won't work." Of course, we didn't have just one community committee; we had four or five active subcommittees and dozens of passionately engaged individuals. Within that kind of stakeholder structure, which we needed to move our ambitious exhibition forward, who makes the final decisions? Where does authority reside? How do you avoid getting bogged down? How do you make the right decisions?

How *9066* navigated past these many challenges—not to mention how we managed to pilot the museum ship given our own inexperience—is the subject for another case study, at another time. The point is that we opened our doors to the community, experimented with making the gallery a safe space for dialogue, and succeeded beyond our expectations. The exhibition drew more than 50,000 visitors to our small facility over a seven-month run and brought national acclaim to a once-quiet neighborhood cultural institution.

This project affirmed for us the power of exhibitions where the objects themselves are linked to stories and issues. On another level, the *9066* exhibition prepared our institution, in the chilling post-9/11 era, to develop a number of strong partnerships between the Japanese-American community and the Arab-American and South Asian communities, which are now living in the shadow of recurring problems of racial profiling and abuses of civil liberties.

Wing Luke was emboldened to use *9066* as the working model for every exhibition to follow. Through what we call our New Dialogues initiative, we now create, usually in the span of several months, dynamic interactive exhibitions on contemporary issues in a small gallery space. Young people and community activists are the backbone of this fresh approach.

In recent years, our profession has begun evolving a vocabulary for the kind of exhibition that *9066* and New Dialogues represents—exhibitions that serve as creative vessels for discussion of contemporary issues, community building, and social action. At the Wing Luke, we call them "community response" exhibitions. During the American civil rights movement, African-American churches were the catalyst and conveners of the masses in the struggle to eradicate segregation. They were the "community response" agents. Today, in like manner, museums, as respected educational institutions, also have the power to serve as "community response" agents. They have the power to shape public opinion, promote tolerance, advocate for social justice, and help improve the quality of life for community residents.

The Wing Luke Asian Museum isn't the only museum looking at ways to remake the gallery into a space for "animating democracy." In an era that the American Association of

Museums has aptly dubbed the era of "Museums and Communities," all museums are moving in the same direction, including art museums that have—in the opinion of many in the profession—been the slowest to change because of a traditional curatorial bias toward letting art "speak for itself," without the "intrusion" of interpretive materials.

This publication provides reflective case studies of exhibitions at The Andy Warhol Museum in Pittsburgh, The Jewish Museum in New York City, and Henry Art Gallery at the University of Washington, Seattle. Each institution experimented with its own version of a "dialogue-based" exhibition, employing artwork and artists to interpret controversial topics.

The Andy Warhol Museum's exhibition, *Without Sanctuary*, consisted of powerful and graphic photographs and postcards of lynchings in the United States. The exhibition was used as a springboard for discussion of race, bias, and bigotry. At The Jewish Museum, *Mirroring Evil: Nazi Imagery/Recent Art* featured controversial and powerful artworks by younger artists exploring the "forbidden character" of the Holocaust perpetrators. Henry Art Gallery created *Gene(sis): Contemporary Art Explores Human Genomics*, a national touring exhibition on the implications of human genetic research on human life and understanding.

Each institution invested much time in developing community partners, with varying degrees of success. Each institution struggled to find an appropriate curatorial voice for the exhibition while simultaneously figuring out how to present differing viewpoints in the gallery, a delicate balance. Each museum faced some degree of public controversy—and dealing with community outrage is still very uncomfortable terrain for most museums. In short, each institution came face to face with the practical reality of re-imagining the museum as a "public space for private reflection made public," in the words of one of the essayists.

These case studies look at how three museums dealt with core challenges inherent to this quest: How do we build workable relationships with artists and other community members? What kind of interpretation should emerge in the gallery? How do we develop sustainable community partnerships and public programs? How do we work with marginalized groups? How do we move beyond preaching to the choir? How do we create a visitor experience that will challenge, but not alienate; educate, but not bore; inspire wonder, but not passivity? How can we use memory and experience not as a passport to the past but as our eyes to the future?

At most museums, the pace of institutional change is still slowed by old habits, timid thinking, and the absence of live connections to social activists, community leaders, artists, and youth—individuals who situate themselves in the laboratory of "here and now." As museums begin to grow these relationships, exhibitions will be judged not simply by the masterful art or evocative objects held up for view, but by the quality of interpretation and the power to spark vibrant dialogue and action inside and outside the walls of the institution.

Ron Chew
Wing Luke Asian Museum

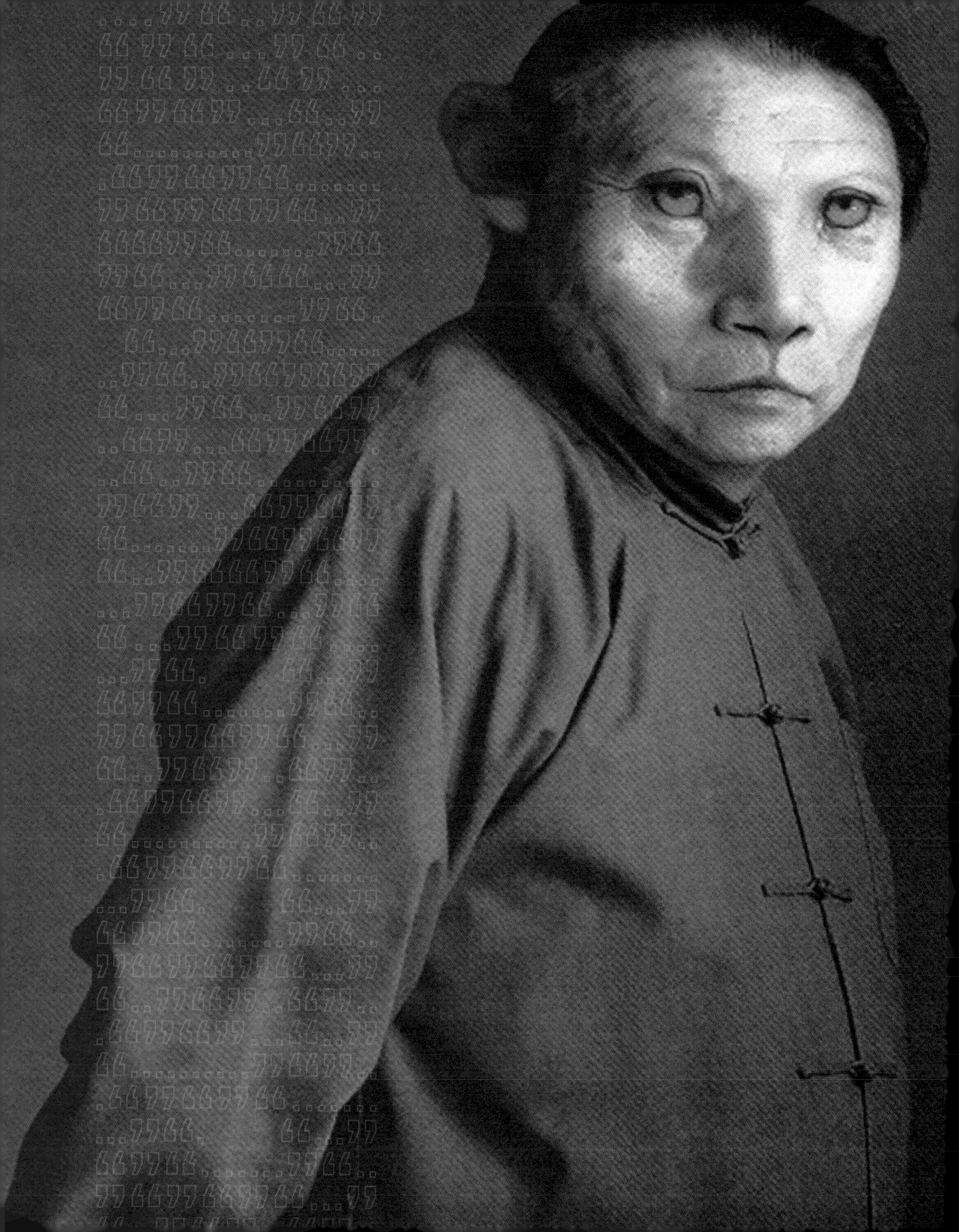

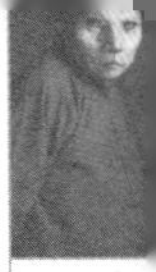

1 Henry Art Gallery

GENE(SIS): CONTEMPORARY ART EXPLORES HUMAN GENOMICS

LYNN E. STERN

Daniel Lee, Juror No. 6 (Leopard Spirit), *1994. Courtesy of the artist.*

PREFACE

In April 2002, on the heels of the Human Genome Project's historic announcement about the completion of a human genome "rough draft" and the publication of its initial analysis by scientists, Seattle's Henry Art Gallery ("the Henry") opened *Gene(sis): Contemporary Art Explores Human Genomics*, a national touring exhibition that explores the implications of human genome research on human life and understanding. *Gene(sis)* brings together more than 50 works of recent and new artwork representing artists' explorations and imaginings of the social, ethical, and economic ramifications of genetic and genome research. To spur dialogue among Puget Sound residents about the provocative and potentially polarizing issues the *Gene(sis)* artwork raises, the Henry, together with its project partners and community collaborators, devised and implemented a multifaceted, cross-disciplinary series of public programs in conjunction with its exhibition. In doing so, the Henry created a "space" for public discourse around a timely and controversial civic issue for Seattle area residents: what is the meaning and impact of current genetic research with regard to our everyday lives?

Through the *Gene(sis)* project, the Henry sought to harness the power of contemporary visual art to elucidate and provoke dialogue about new developments in the science of

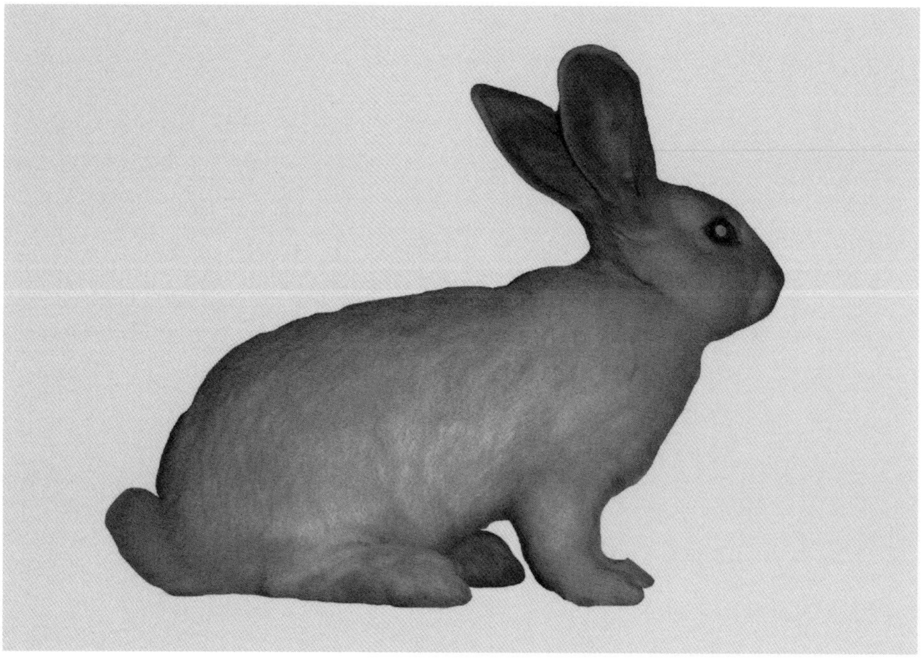

Eduardo Kac, GFP Bunny, *2000. Alba, the fluorescent rabbit. Courtesy Julia Friedman Gallery.*

human genomics. The Henry employed a range of approaches and formats to spark discussion on these themes within a gallery setting and at public programs throughout the city. The Henry's exploration of various dialogue methods raised key questions about dialogue concepts and practices: What new innovations can be brought to conducting dialogue about art and, in this case, "controversial art?" How does art function as dialogue between artist and viewer? Does the viewer's experience in grappling with the ideas evoked by a work of art constitute civic dialogue? And what do existing curatorial and education practices have to offer when designing opportunities for civic dialogue?

WHO OWNS YOUR DNA?
ARTISTS PROBE THE HUMAN GENOME'S IMPLICATIONS

> *A powerful statement can be made if you go in the trenches and you appropriate the same [scientific] tools. And what you say with those tools is a completely different diction, a completely different message, a completely different everything. You show that these tools are the instrument of fantasy. The tools are invested with ideological value. They come from a certain view of the world, but these are not issues that science is interested in talking about... This is the job of the artist. What artists do is social awareness, this inventiveness, this fantasy.*[1]
>
> *—Eduardo Kac, artist*

[1] Eduardo Kac, as referenced in the article "Art Ponders Genome Implications," by Deidtra Henderson, *Boston Globe.* April 7, 2002.

Henry Art Gallery: A Laboratory for Emerging Art Forms

The University of Washington's Henry Art Gallery in Seattle is a nationally recognized center for the exploration and advancement of contemporary art, design, and visual culture.

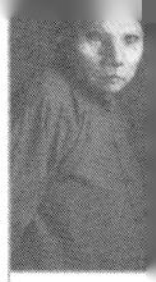

Founded in 1927 as the state of Washington's first public art museum, the Henry has carved out a unique profile as an institution dedicated to pioneering the yet-to-be-charted frontiers of contemporary art. Central to the Henry's mission is its role as a catalyst for the creation of new work in the visual arts, placing special emphasis on commissioning works by artists who are exploring the intersection of art and technology. To advance that vision, the Henry built a state-of-the-art gallery in 1997 to accommodate artists' experimentation in the embryonic fields of video and digital media. In the words of the Henry's director, Richard Andrews, the gallery serves "as a place for experimentation and to house developing art forms, even though we are not even sure yet what those forms will be."

Recognizing the power of contemporary art to provoke, challenge, and articulate fresh ideas around complex and often polarizing social issues, the Henry is equally committed to engaging audiences in the powerful experience of artistic innovation. Through a dynamic mix of exhibitions, education programs, and public events, the Henry positions itself as public forum that helps communities in the Puget Sound region deepen their understanding of and response to ideas evoked by cutting edge art.

With anticipation building around the release of the human genome "working draft," the Henry was keenly aware of the Gene(sis) *project as a prime opportunity to focus public attention on the social, ethical, and economic ramifications of biogenetics.*

Evolution of the *Gene(sis)* Project (1999–2000)

With its finger on the pulse of artistic experimentation, the Henry was one of a handful of art museums whose artistic activity at the end of the 20th century reflected on and responded to recent trends in genetic and genomic research. That artistic exploration was spurred in large part by the formation in 1990 of the Human Genome Project (HGP), an international consortium of scientific laboratories engaged in a 15-year effort to map and sequence the human genome—the totality of genetic material that makes us human. In deciphering the code of human life, HGP held the promise of unraveling the mysteries of how the human body grows and functions. Knowledge harvested from the project would reap untold benefits for humankind, revolutionizing the fields of medicine, biology, and psychology by offering new tools for improved diagnosis of disease, detection of genetic predispositions to disease, and rational drug design and gene therapies. Its non-medical applications would contribute to a greater understanding of human evolution and anthropology, and lead to advances in the fields of DNA forensics, agriculture, and environmental protection, among others.

But cracking the secrets of life also raises a thicket of social, legal, and ethical questions. Many argue that genetic information and its uses are especially vulnerable to adverse refraction through the lenses of power, fear, social prejudice, and economic interest. Will the gains that promise to heal diseases also give rise to designer babies, cloning, and genetically modified "Frankenfood?" How will issues of privacy and fair use of genetic material be negotiated in the public policy arena? Will HGP's findings revive the 19th century "science" of eugenics and foster new forms of genetic discrimination? And how will the commercialization of knowledge—such as the race among for-profit biotech firms to patent and copyright DNA information—affect the accessibility of data and materials for public health applications?

HGP and its broader implications have special resonance for the city of Seattle. A number of Seattle-based research institutions, including the University of Washington's Human Genome Center, were members of HGP's international coalition. Seattle has also staked its economic future on the region's burgeoning biotech industry, making significant capital and infrastructure investments to raise Seattle's profile as a leading hub for biotech research and innovation.

"A legitimate question to ask is: What can an art museum contribute—through its exhibition and public programs—to the larger discourse about the implications of human genomics on our everyday lives?"

As the completion of the human genome "working draft" drew near, an increasing number of artists were creating genome-related work that grappled with the cultural and ethical implications of genetic engineering. In doing so, these artists were taking up the tools and materials of genetic researchers, turning their studios into "laboratories" to pursue these investigations.

Intrigued by this artistic trend and the genetic research that spawned it, the Henry's Associate Curator Robin Held began a series of conversations in 1999 with artists, scientists, historians, and biotechnology industry representatives to solicit their interest in organizing an exhibition that would explore HGP's implications in light of present-day notions about human life and identity. That same year, with a planning grant from the National Endowment for the Arts, the Henry convened a working group of interested parties for a roundtable planning session to define the basic goals of collaboration and explore possible exhibition themes. The positive tenor of that gathering inspired the Henry to take this unprecedented cross-disciplinary endeavor to the next level. "There was a high level of conversation about possible collaborations, enthusiasm, good will, and discourse," recalls Held, "and we knew we had to do something with that energy."[2]

[2] *Seattle Magazine*, April 2002.

With input and guidance from the *Gene(sis)* working group, the Henry fleshed out a three-year project that would culminate in *Gene(sis): Contemporary Art Explores Human Genomics*, a major touring exhibition featuring recent and newly commissioned genome-themed artwork. To facilitate the project's planning and execution as a collective effort, it was structured to loosely mirror the laboratory model used in international efforts to investigate human genome sequencing. As Held describes that process, "Artists, scientific collaborators, and museum professionals worked simultaneously in their own corners of the country, remained in regular contact via e-mail correspondence and phone conversations, and held small group meetings."[3] In that same vein, three new works commissioned by the Henry would be created by artists in collaboration with experts from various scientific fields.

[3] Robin Held, *Generating Gene(sis): A Contemporary Art Exhibition for the "Genomic Age,"* 5.

What Can an Art Museum Contribute to Public Discourse About the Human Genome?

With anticipation building around the release of the human genome "working draft," the Henry was keenly aware of the *Gene(sis)* project as a prime opportunity to focus public attention on the social, ethical, and economic ramifications of biogenetics. In bridging the divergent spheres of art and science, as Robin Held explains, the Henry saw the exhibition's potential to activate citizens' engagement in a broader public discourse about the implications of genome research on their lives.

> We're trying to encourage dialogue, rather than keep art and science divided. One goal I have is for people to see that it isn't a done deal. Citizens can be part of the conversation in genomics. Artists, naturally, don't all agree on biotech issues, and several viewpoints are presented. But what is shown mirrors the potential impacts on our daily lives, and that's worth talking about.[4]

[4] *Seattle Magazine*, April 2002.

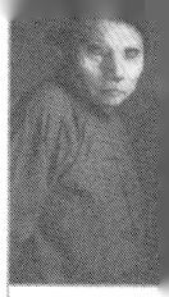

To achieve that vision, the Henry mapped out an ambitious roster of public programs and events in conjunction with the exhibition, aimed at stimulating dialogue about these concerns among a broad cross section of Puget Sound residents. As an affiliate institution of the University of Washington (UW), the Henry was well-placed to harness the rich resources of UW's academic community and bring a cross-disciplinary approach to the planning and execution of *Gene(sis)* programming. To extend the *Gene(sis)* project's reach and impact beyond the UW campus, the Henry planned to partner with a range of Seattle-based organizations—from cultural institutions and arts groups to scientific institutes and public health agencies—to produce an eclectic mix of *Gene(sis)*-related activities.

In taking on the *Gene(sis)* project, the Henry sought to spur discussion about one of the Seattle community's most complex and possibly controversial civic issues: what is the meaning and impact of current genetic research on our everyday lives? In doing so, the Henry confronted a set of institutional and philosophical challenges that it had never before faced, and had to ask itself some tough questions: What is the role of contemporary art in generating new ideas and in serving as a catalyst for discussion on civic issues? Does a "science-based" exhibition have a place in a contemporary art museum? And how can the Henry serve as a public forum for dialogue about difficult and potentially polarizing civic issues? Robin Held framed the Henry's challenges in this way: "The scope of this project is clearly beyond the usual curatorial mandate of an art museum. A legitimate question to ask is: What can an art museum contribute—through its exhibition and public programs—to the larger discourse about the implications of human genomics on our everyday lives?"[5]

Artistic and Dialogic Intentions

Support from Animating Democracy in 2000 provided the Henry the opportunity to realize the *Gene(sis)* project's wide-ranging public programs component, as well as to test its assumptions about the exhibition as a stimulus for civic dialogue and its own role in carving out a civic "space"—a public forum within the museum walls and outside them—for public discussion and debate.

"Visual metaphors in contemporary art can provide new ways of approaching this important civic issue and offer the general public a point of entry into these questions."

The Henry's primary artistic intent for the project was to organize a major touring exhibition of recent and newly commissioned works that would elucidate ideas and provoke dialogue about new developments in the science of human genomics. Underlying that intent was the Henry's assumption that contemporary art could make a unique contribution to a broader understanding of the complex ideas surrounding biotechnology and genomics. As one Henry staff member put it, "Visual metaphors in contemporary art can provide new ways of approaching this important civic issue and offer the general public a point of entry into these questions."[6] The Henry's second artistic interest was to explore through the *Gene(sis)* project the intersection of fine art and hard science. That artistic inquiry would be investigated most directly through the Henry's commissioning of three new works that artists would create in collaboration with scientists from the field of genomics.

In articulating the project's dialogic goals, the Henry envisioned the *Gene(sis)* project as a potent vehicle for increasing public awareness and involvement relative to human genome issues among a broad cross-section of Puget Sound residents. To advance that goal, the Henry undertook dialogue activities at two levels. On one level, the Henry focused on the experience and response of audiences to the *Gene(sis)* exhibition as a form of dialogue,

[5] Held, 2.

[6] Henry Art Gallery application to Animating Democracy, 2000. Unless otherwise noted, quotes are drawn from the Henry reports and supplemental materials to Animating Democracy.

modifying a variety of interpretive approaches to the visual arts experience to provoke questions and discussion about the artwork. On another level, the Henry employed a broad public engagement strategy to spur dialogue about the issues raised by *Gene(sis)* artwork. That approach was largely realized through the project's multi-faceted public program component, with activities that ranged from small gallery discussions and artists' talks to public symposia and other off-site events in collaboration with Seattle community partners. To expand the reach of dialogue activities in Seattle and cities on the national tour, the Henry created a teachers' curriculum guide and an exhibition "toolbox" aimed at encouraging subsequent *Gene(sis)* venues to replicate and expand the Henry's dialogue activities in their own communities.

Through Animating Democracy, the Henry also investigated in a systematic way the experience and responses of audiences to the *Gene(sis)* exhibition and/or participation in public programs, with the goal of gauging changes in the audiences' awareness and understanding of the issues involved in human genetics and biotechnology research. The Henry worked with Animating Democracy staff and consultants to develop an evaluation framework for that inquiry and analysis.

Finally, the premise of the Henry's orientation to arts-based dialogue would be based on the notion that the *Gene(sis)* artwork, either in its original form or in reproduction, would serve as the catalyst for dialogue. The Henry's curatorial staff provided substantial background and wall text for the viewer. Still, the Henry presented *Gene(sis)* in a neutral way—without an agenda or point of view—so as to provide audiences with the opportunity to make up their own minds about the provocative issues raised by the artwork.

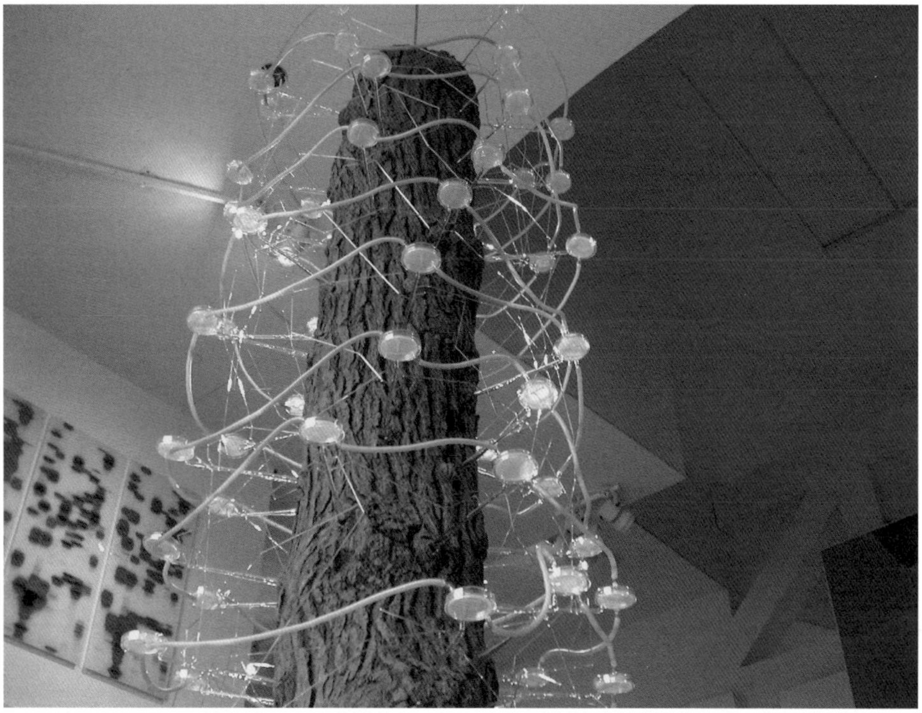

Jill Reynolds, Family Tree II, *2002. Courtesy of the artist.*

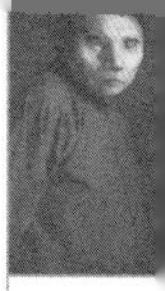

IN THE PUBLIC EYE AND UNDER THE MICROSCOPE: HENRY ART GALLERY ENTERS INTO THE FRAY OF THE GENOMICS DEBATE

> *Scientific revolutions may start with dry, objective data, but their ultimate impact depends on human interpretation in a societal context. Scientific milestones set off a search, often a struggle, for the metaphors and images that will be used to connect the findings with our daily lives... [T]he struggle over the meaning of the human genome is already under way. The language and imagery will be important because it will shape society's choices in the coming decades.*[7]
>
> —*Dr. Eric S. Lander*

In June 2000, midway through the organization of the *Gene(sis)* project, the Human Genome Project and Celera Genomics, a private firm, jointly announced the completion of a "working draft" of the human genome. This stunning news intensified public scrutiny and debate, in the United States and globally, about genomic research. It also brought a renewed sense of urgency and import to the Henry's role, through the *Gene(sis)* project, as a catalyst for public discussion about the implications of the human genome. As one Henry staff person recalls, "The issue not only became more concrete for the public—suddenly the word 'genome' appeared regularly in the popular press—but also more polarized. The Henry located itself in the center of this speculation with the *Gene(sis)* exhibition and by developing and co-sponsoring more public programs than the museum had ever conducted. We were suddenly in the public eye and under the microscope."

"The issue not only became more concrete for the public—suddenly the word 'genome' appeared regularly in the popular press—but also more polarized.... We were suddenly in the public eye and under the microscope."

Primary *Gene(sis)* Partners and Roles

Against this backdrop, the Henry convened a two-day gathering, *Forum on Art and Human Genomics*, in December 2000 as a follow-up to the 1999 planning session. The forum was designed to present and elicit feedback on the three new works commissioned by the Henry for the *Gene(sis)* exhibition: Paul Vanouse's "Relative Velocity Inscription Device," Shawn Brixey and Richard Rinehart's "Chimera Obscura," and Jill Reynold's "Family Tree II." The forum was also intended to revisit key issues identified in the 1999 planning session, revise and refine them, and select five core themes for the focus of the Henry's public programs.

In addition to artists, scholars, and scientists, attendees at the forum included key Henry staff and the primary community partners responsible for the development and production of the *Gene(sis)* public program. The Henry team included Robin Held, *Gene(sis)* curator; Sara Pasti, director of curatorial affairs; Tamara Moats, curator of education; and Felicia Gonzalez, foundation and government relations manager. The Henry's four primary community partners were Nancy Pearl, executive director of the Washington Center for the Book at the Seattle Public Library (WCB), an organization that broadens and deepens appreciation for literature through book discussions and other literary and humanities programs; Margit Dementi, associate director of UW's Walter Chapin Simpson Center for the Humanities, which supports interdisciplinary activities in the humanities; Richard Francois, director of development and community relations at the Seattle Biomedical Research Institute (SBRI), a nonprofit research institute that also promotes broad-based education about the value of fundamental research and improved global health; and Maynard Olson, director of the UW Human Genome Center, one of the nation's leading research institutions dedicated to the sequencing of the human genome.

[7] Eric S. Lander, "In Wake of Genetic Revolution, Questions about Its Meaning," *New York Times*, September 12, 2000.

Forum participants generated five core themes that provided the conceptual framework for developing public programs in conjunction with the exhibition's presentation at the Henry:

- "Paradigms Lost and Found," the potential impact of recent genome research on notions of self, family, race, and ethnicity;
- "Designer Bodies," the implications of genetic engineering and genetic intervention on disease treatment, human biodiversity, and species boundaries;
- "Bioethics and Public Policy," implications of the control of genetic information in creating definitions of normalcy and discrimination;
- "Public Conceptions and Misconceptions about Human Genomics," the influence of education, media, and the development of language on the public understanding of human genomics; and
- "The Concept of Aesthetic Elegance in Art and Science," concepts and processes shared by art and science.

Based on the five key themes outlined at the December forum, the Henry and its primary community partners pooled their collective experience and resources to devise and facilitate an engaging, wide-ranging series of dialogue activities that would appeal to diverse constituencies. As an affiliate of the Seattle Public Library, WCB was well-positioned to introduce these themes into the larger public realm through dialogue activities and informational resources geared to lay audiences. Modeled on the success of its nationally acclaimed *If All of Seattle Read the Same Book* project, WCB would host monthly discussion groups throughout the *Gene(sis)* exhibition on selected books at the library's 25 branches. It would also develop a reading list and study guides on *Gene(sis)*-related books for use by library-sponsored and independent book clubs throughout Seattle. As co-host of a symposium to be held as part of the exhibition's 2002 opening, the Simpson Center would serve as liaison to UW faculty and staff, identifying and securing participation for the symposium from a broad cross-section of the academic community. Concurrent with the exhibition, the Simpson Center would also offer UW undergraduate and graduate students two cross-disciplinary, team-taught courses on *Gene(sis)*-related themes. Drawing on its network in the biotechnology field, SBRI would identify and provide access to business leaders, policymakers, ethicists, and international representatives of social sciences for the development of the public programs component.

In addition to the *Gene(sis)* project's primary partners, a number of community collaborators planned to develop programs that would complement and make reference to *Gene(sis)* artwork and public program themes. These organizations included Richard Hugo House; a nonprofit literary center for practicing writers; the Fred Hutchinson Cancer Research Center; Sustainable Science Institute, a nonprofit dedicated to improving public health worldwide; Cornish College for the Arts; and the Washington State Board of Health.

The Henry Brings the DNA Debate to Life: The 2002 Premiere of *Gene(sis)*

Gene(sis): Contemporary Art Explores Human Genomics, which premiered at the Henry on April 6, 2002, brought together more than 50 recent and new works by 28 U.S. and European artists. In grappling with the human genome and its implications, the artists had explored nearly every avenue of artmaking—paintings, drawings, photographs, performance, Internet-based art, and installation works—and employed a range of materials,

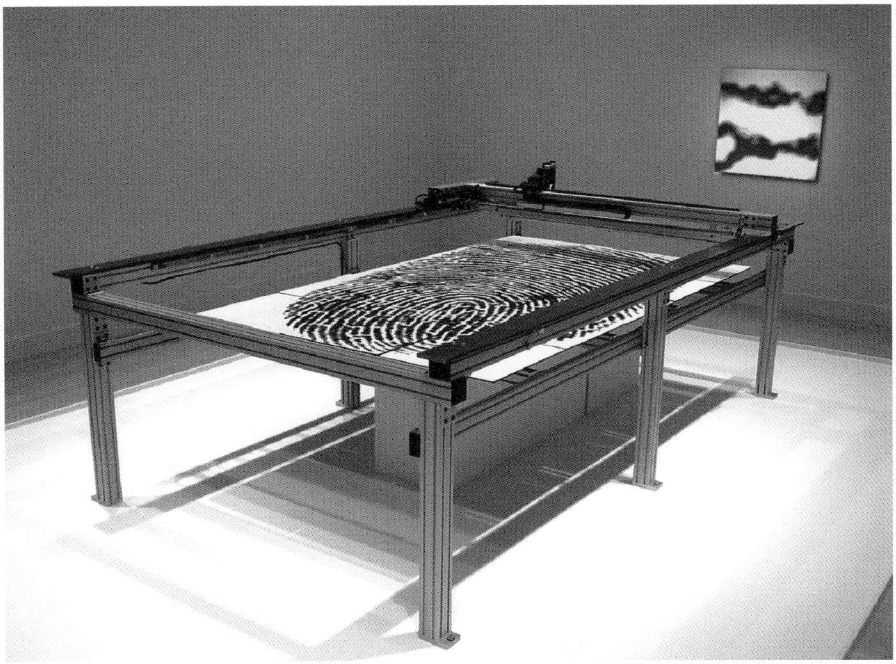

Shawn Brixey and Richard Rinehart, Chimera Obscura, *2002. Courtesy of the artists.*

from microscopes and Petri dishes to paper coffee cups and frogs preserved in glass jars. A number of works were interactive, allowing museum visitors to influence the process of genetic mutation and observe the results. From glowing bacteria to "manimals" and genes for sale, each piece touched on important issues surrounding the remarkable developments in human genomic research over the past decade.

As described by Robin Held in her introductory essay to the exhibition, *Gene(sis)* was organized into four thematic sections: SEQUENCE, work that explores the rhetoric and media representations of genomics; BOUNDARY, artists' investigations of the now permeable boundaries between species; SPECIMEN, work that engages questions of DNA ownership, personal privacy, and the management of genetic information; and SUBJECT, artists' re-imaginings of individual subjectivity, family, and human "nature" in the wake of recent genomic developments.

The new works generated by the *Gene(sis)* project formed the focal point of the exhibition. Jill Reynold's *Family Tree II*, in the thematic section SUBJECT, is a tree-like installation wrapped in a web of glass rods connected to each other by small Petri dishes that contain growing yeast. Highlighting the interconnectedness of life, the work illuminates one of the earliest insights garnered from human genome research: the human genome shares surprising similarities with the genomes of other species, such as the mouse, roundworm, fruit fly, and yeast. Paul Vanouse's "Relative Inscription Device," also in the SUBJECT section, is a multimedia installation employing game theory to compare and contrast historical issues of eugenics and contemporary notions of human biodiversity (or "race"). Using DNA samples from his family members, Vanouse constructed a "race" about race, in which a genetic sequencing gel serves as a track for the competition as the genetic species "fight" for the lead. In "Chimera Obscura," new media artists Shawn Brixey and Richard Rinehart created a large-scale maze in the image of a human thumbprint that can be navigated remotely by Internet visitors. As a key work under the section of SEQUENCE, this work reflects the artists' understanding of the process of mapping of the human genome.

Another new work featured at the *Gene(sis)* opening was the U.S. premiere of "Gen Terra" by the Critical Art Ensemble (CAE), a collective of five artists dedicated to exploring the intersections between art, technology, critical theory, and political activism. Described by CAE as "a theater of transgenics," "Gen Terra" employs genetic materials and lab practices with the direct participation of the audience in order to examine fears about recent transgenic initiatives. Lab-coated technicians invite audiences to play "transgenetic roulette" with Petri dishes on a revolving platform, potentially releasing benign transgenic bacteria into the air. Audience members are also encouraged to make and store their own transgenic bacteria.

In the wake of the September 11th tragedy and subsequent anthrax scares, "Gen Terra" proved to be one of *Gene(sis)*'s most provocative and controversial pieces. Concerns by the public about possible exposure to transgenic bacteria required sensitive negotiations between the Henry, UW's Environmental Safety Department, and the Office of Risk Management in order to present the work—a deliberative process that played out in real life some of the fears and anxieties about biological agents that "Gen Terra" aimed to evoke and interrogate.

Engaging Multiple Approaches and Formats to Spark Dialogue

Concurrent with the exhibition's four-month run, the Henry, its partners, and community collaborators presented a robust public programs schedule. Many of these programs aimed to spark discussion on various levels about the exhibition and the issues involved in genetic research. In the public programs component, the organizers sought to explore the subject matter through multiple lenses—literature, film, and dance, among others—and made use of a variety of formats, such as hands-on demonstrations, symposia, readings, public meetings, gallery talks, and formal presentations with facilitated dialogues sessions. To plan and facilitate the public programs component, the Henry hired a half-time staff person, Bridget Nowlin, who served as *Gene(sis)* program coordinator and worked closely with Curator of Education Tamara Moats.

Lerman's choreography of each participant's emotional response—in the physical form of an individual's gesture—transformed the very private experience of viewing the artwork into a public communal one.

The key activities illustrate the breadth of *Gene(sis)*-related programs.

***The Permeable Membrane: A Dialogue on Art and Issues* (March 23, 2002), presented in cooperation with the Cornish College for the Arts.** Choreographer/dancer Liz Lerman and members of the Dance Exchange conducted a Critical Response Process workshop, a movement-based approach that engaged participants in an exploration of the layers of meaning and response to artist Eduardo Kac's *Gene(sis)*.

***Paradigms Lost and Found: The Implications of the Human Genome Project* (April 5–7, 2002), co-sponsored by the Walter Chapin Simpson Center for the Humanities.** This two-day symposium brought together *Gene(sis)* artists, scientists, and scholars for presentations and panel discussions that explored the potential social

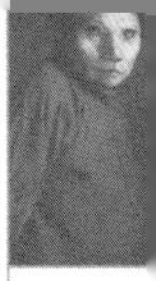

and ethical impact of genetic research. Panels were interspersed with 30- to 40-minute "dialogue sessions" led by a professional dialogue facilitator. During the lunch break, audience members could take a 15-minute guided tour of the exhibition.

Washington State Board of Health Genetics Task Force Public Meeting (April 12, 2002). The day-long public hearing presented testimony from leading scientists, public health experts, and biotechnology representatives on three issues: Future Directions of Academic and Basic Research in Human Genetics; Future Directions of Genomics in Public Health Practice; and Private Ventures in Genomic Diagnostic and Treatment Technologies. The meeting also invited public comment on genetics-related privacy and/or discrimination issues. Meeting participants and task force members toured the *Gene(sis)* exhibition.

Facilitated Book Group Readings (April 16 and May 9, 2002). Through its network of more than 150 book groups, WCB explored two titles in association with *Gene(sis)*: *Frankenstein* by Mary Shelley and *Mendel's Dwarf* by Simon Mawer.

***Gene(sis): A Bridge Between Art and Science in the Classroom* (April 16, 2001)** This was an evening for educators to tour the *Gene(sis)* exhibition and discuss the use of the *Gene(sis)* teacher curriculum guide assembled by the Henry.

***Gene(sis)* Town Hall Meeting at Town Hall Seattle (May 4, 2002), co-sponsored by Town Hall Seattle.** The meeting featured presentations on the future of human genetic research by Lee Hartwell, 2001 Nobel Laureate, UW genetics professor, and president of the Fred Hutchinson Cancer Research; and Leroy Hood, geneticist and director of Seattle's Institute for Systems Biology. Presentations were followed by a discussion led by a professional dialogue facilitator.

***Genetic Screenings* Film Series (April–May 2002), organized by the Pacific Film Archive at the University of California, Berkeley.** This six-part series offered a cinematic survey of features, shorts, and documentary films that have engaged the human genome either as focus or foil. The series also included the premiere at the Seattle International Film Festival of *Teknolust* (2002), a cyber-comedy about a female scientist (Tilda Swinton) who clones three selves.

***Author Series: A Conversation on Bioethics and Public Policy* (April 12 and May 24, 2002), co-sponsored by UW Forum at the Evans School and the University Book Store.** These events featured discussions with the authors on two new books on genomics: *Redesigning Humans: Choosing Our Children's Genes* by Dr. Gregory Stock, and *Mapping Human History: Discovering the Past Through Our Genes* by Steve Olson.

***DNA Precipitation Display* (April–August 2004), organized by the Fred Hutchinson Cancer Research Center and the Sustainable Science Institute.** This interactive display, offered regularly throughout the exhibition's run in the Henry's Educational Studio, allowed visitors to participate in a demonstration of the precipitation of DNA.

***Inquiry Through Writing* Classes (January–June 2002).** The Richard Hugo House offered three creative writing classes: *The Art of Science*, in which writers examined the similarities of scientific and artistic processes; *Writing the Thing*, which encouraged writers to focus on the "thingly" side of human nature, DNA; and *Sequence, Syntax, Language, and Perception*, in which writers explored the question, "Are we made up of genes or stories?" Spring classes included visits to the *Gene(sis)* exhibition.

University of Washington Courses (spring quarter 2002), sponsored by the UW Walter Chapin Simpson Center for the Humanities. Two cross-disciplinary, team-taught courses were offered to UW undergraduates and graduate students: *In Vivo: Traversing Scientific and Artistic Observations of Life Science*; and *Science, Technology, and the Body*.

VISUAL THINKING STRATEGY ADAPTED FOR DIALOGUE

A questioning strategy for artist Catherine Chalmers' *Transgenic Mice* (2002), excerpted from the Henry's *Gene(sis)* teacher curriculum guide, offers a snapshot of how the Henry's version of VTS guides the viewer(s) in a dialogue around the artwork, its interpretation, and the ethical issues raised by the work. Chalmers documents the production of genetically engineered mice, a burgeoning industry fueled by recent genetic discoveries. Her photographs spotlight the "mouse ranch" industry, calling into question the ethics of animal research. Suggested discussion questions for this piece include:

Art:

- Describe what you see in these photographs. How many mice? What size? Texture? Shape? Color?
- Note the way in which the artist has framed the mice, and their size within the frame. How does this affect the portrayal of the mice?
- Note the manner in which they have been photographed (glossy paper, professionally lit). How does this style (glossy, blown-up, closely cropped, highly detailed) influence your response to the image?

Interpretation:

- Are these mouse portraits emotional or scientific? Why or why not?
- What do you think is the artist's intent by photographing these mice?
- Does she seem for or against animal experimentation? What clues do the artwork give you to support your opinion?

Ethics:

- How are these mice normal? Abnormal?
- Is it right to use animals in research to explore human illness and its treatments?
- If they are not used for research, what about the humans who might suffer and die because of lack of treatment?
- Let's say insects or yeast were used for research. Would you feel differently?
- Is it any more ethical to experiment on one type of living creature than another?
- Where do we draw the line?
- As an artist, Chalmers also benefits indirectly from the research these mice undergo (she presumably makes money from her art, and gets notoriety). What are the issues she as an artist should be concerned about when working with such subject matter?

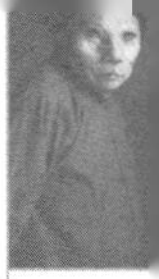

***Gene(sis)* as a Laboratory for Dialogue**

The Henry's participation in Animating Democracy constituted the museum's first formal encounter with concepts of dialogue and civic dialogue practice in its work. Embracing the spirit of Animating Democracy as a laboratory, the Henry committed itself to learning and experimenting with selected arts-based dialogue concepts and practices. It adapted standard museum education methodologies, extending its capacity to engage people in dialogue within the gallery setting. The Henry also tried out dialogue methodologies that might be considered "unconventional" within the context of a visual arts museum. Henry Director Richard Andrews notes that, through its participation in Animating Democracy, "the Henry grew and stretched beyond our institutional parameters and beyond our comfort zone. [The *Gene(sis)* project] opened the museum to exploration, play, dialogue, and performance in ways that other projects have not made possible." As host to Animating Democracy's May 2002 Learning Exchange, the Henry provided fellow Lab participants[8] with an opportunity to experience first-hand a number of dialogue approaches employed by the museum in the *Gene(sis)* project.

[8] Cultural organizations who participated in Animating Democracy were part of the Animating Democracy Lab. The Lab encouraged experimentation in arts- and humanities-based civic dialogue through the organizations' project work and enabled cultural leaders, artists, and dialogue and community partners to come together for mutual learning purposes in gatherings called Learning Exchanges.

In exploring audience experience and response to the *Gene(sis)* artwork, the Henry brought to bear several interpretive approaches that were used in guided gallery talks for general audiences and educator-led visits for student groups. Building on the strength of the museum's educational department, the Henry developed and documented in its *Gene(sis)* teacher curriculum guide a participatory viewing experience adapted from the Visual Thinking Strategy (VTS), a method of inquiry developed by the Museum of Modern Art. As the Henry's Education Curator Tamara Moats explained at the Seattle Learning Exchange, VTS draws out viewer response through inquiry and explores information about an artwork meaningful to the viewer. Described by the Henry staff as an "interactive looking experience," VTS initiates dialogue by posing simple questions that encourage viewers to bring their own personal associations, stories, and interpretations to the work. This questioning strategy leads viewers in progressive steps to explore the complex and sometimes disturbing ideas embedded in the work. (See sidebar.)

At the Seattle Learning Exchange, the Henry staff demonstrated its version of VTS for Lab participants. Selma Holo, museum studies scholar and director of the University of California Fisher Gallery, describes how the Henry tour leaders' questioning strategy gradually led to the ethical and moral dilemmas at the heart of *Gene(sis)*:

> This approach allowed visitors to verbalize their concerns generated by the most radical art and its attendant scientific ideas. The VTS method was handled flexibly and generously, in that the tour leaders explained the basic scientific concepts so that an informed conversation could begin. Simultaneously Socratic and teacherly, the Henry version of VTS elicited heartfelt and smart responses, and was able to handle both the nervousness and curiosity generated by the disturbing images on display. Questions about the ethics and morality of both artists and scientists who undertake work with this material began to emerge and a level of inquiry about the important issues raised by the curatorial thesis was encouraged.[9]

[9] Selma Holo, "Conducting Civic Dialogue: A Challenging Role for Museums," (Washington, DC: Americans for the Arts, 2002), www.AmericansForTheArts.org/AnimatingDemocracy

In contrast to Holo's observations, some Language Exchange participants expressed concern that the Henry's version of the VTS method merely led participants to intended conclusions rather than creating a setting for a viewer's own discovery about the artwork. They suggested that this questioning strategy assumes there are "right answers" to which a viewer can be guided by asking the right questions.

Another interpretive approach to *Gene(sis)* artwork was offered by *The Permeable Membrane: A Dialogue on Art and Issues*. This workshop, conducted by dancer/choreographer Liz Lerman and several of her company's dancers, incorporated elements of the Critical Response Process (CRP), a multistep format for conducting conversations about art that Lerman originally developed as a way for an artist to engage in dialogue with a group of responders about a work-in-progress. Lerman led workshop participants in a movement-based dialogue exploring meaning and response to Eduardo Kac's *Gene(sis)* installation. Workshop participants experienced elements of CRP combined with techniques that "tap the body's capacity for holding memory and gauging intellectual and emotional reactions." As the Henry notes in its final report to Animating Democracy, this type of movement-based inquiry rarely, if ever, occurs within an art museum setting.

At the Seattle Learning Exchange, Lerman adapted elements of *The Permeable Membrane* to conduct a gallery dialogue around Kac's installation for Learning Exchange participants. In her description of Lerman's gallery dialogue, Selma Holo suggests that the physicality of the process helped individual participants unlock deeper emotional responses to the work. As Holo describes it, Lerman's choreography of each participant's emotional response—in the physical form of an individual's gesture—transformed the very private experience of viewing the artwork into a public communal one.

> [B]ased on participants' experience of Kac's installation, Lerman asked "What was meaningful to you?" Individuals spoke, then, recalling movement and gestures from certain participants' responses, Lerman engaged the group in performing those gestures together, eventually creating an entire movement phrase to music. Harvesting gestures from individual experiences simultaneously created a deeply personal and collective experience in an arts space where collective experience is not the norm. For some, acting out the "angst and tension" that Kac's piece provoked relieved these feelings, making it possible to talk more easily about the issues. For others, the gestures enhanced listening and gave deeper meaning to words.[10]

[10] Ibid.

For *Gene(sis)*-related activities that took place outside the gallery, the Henry adapted conventional formats and techniques to spur discussion around the themes raised by the *Gene(sis)* artwork. In designing the project's public events, such as the symposium and town hall meeting, the Henry placed special emphasis on creating "space" for public dialogue sessions within the program format. The Henry also secured the services of Heather Andersen, a professional dialogue facilitator to lead these sessions and train museum staff and community partners in dialogue facilitation. For example, the *Paradigms Lost and Found* symposium interspersed panel discussions with 30- to 40-minute dialogue sessions led by a professional dialogue facilitator. In structuring the dialogue sessions, a key consideration was how to break out of the standard Q & A format and create an environment that encouraged all members to voice their ideas and concerns. In its

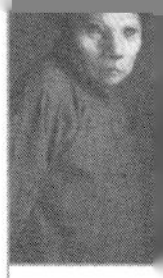

final report to Animating Democracy, the Henry staff explained the thinking behind the symposium's dialogue sessions:

> An important aspect of the symposium was to provide opportunities for the audience to dialogue with both the presenters and one another. The structure for these dialogues was carefully thought out in order to avoid the standard question and answer format. Rather, we facilitated the dialogues so that people would feel comfortable addressing one another as well as the presenter. One way this was achieved was to bring the presenter(s) down from the stage and into the audience. This arrangement stressed the idea that everyone's point of view was equal and all were welcome to share. We also engaged a professional dialogue facilitator for the program and also had her train museum staff on dialogue facilitation so that the format these sessions took was clear and that all could come, listen, and be heard.

In structuring the off-site *Gene(sis)* dialogue activities, the Henry also made a deliberate effort to link these programs to the artwork whenever possible by referencing the work and/or building gallery tours into the format, such as the 15-minute guided tours during the lunch break at *Paradigms Lost and Found*. The symposium utilized the genome theme as the foundation for a broad exploration of topics in which artists and scientists had mutual interest. Panels combined scientists and artists who shared perspectives on the ethics, politics, and social implications of genome research, and the relationship between arts and science. The discussion occasionally referenced the artworks and noted the way that the art both illustrated and challenged genome research and biogenetics. With the exception of artist Eduardo Kac's presentation, specific works were not viewed or specifically discussed in panel sessions. The audience for the event was small, but people fully participated in the discussion.

For the Henry curators, the intent of civic dialogue often appeared to be at odds with their goal of allowing the artwork to "speak for itself," at times creating tension regarding whether the dialogue was driving the art.

The Henry also arranged exhibit tours for writers participating in the Hugo House's Inquiry Through Writing classes. As part of the Genetics Task Force Public Meeting, members of the task force, representatives from the biotech industry, and others testifying at the meeting toured the exhibition as part of the day's agenda—a rare example of injecting contemporary art into a public policy setting.

To articulate dialogue goals during the planning for *Gene(sis)* and later gauge audience experience and response to the *Gene(sis)* exhibition and related public programs, the Henry—in consultation with Animating Democracy's evaluation consultant—developed a detailed logic model that outlined the project's activities, correlating each key activity to desired immediate and long-term outcomes and impacts. The Henry also devised several evaluation tools, such as an exhibition survey questionnaire, and adapted an audience questionnaire developed by Animating Democracy's evaluation coaches.

EMERGENT QUESTIONS AND OUTCOMES

Taken as a whole, the *Gene(sis)* project is a remarkable example of an art museum heralding a timely civic issue of profound social and ethical consequences for its community and marshalling its considerable resources to bring that issue to the forefront of public attention. The project had the cumulative effect of heightening awareness and understanding among

Seattle area residents about the promise and potential hazards that the Human Genome Project holds for our daily lives. By virtue of its three-city tour, the *Gene(sis)* project has also contributed to the national conversation about genomics and genetic exploration. If the meaning of human genome, as geneticist Dr. Eric Lander suggests, will ultimately be determined in the arena of art and culture, then the thought-provoking metaphors and images emanating from the *Gene(sis)* project may well form the basis for our understanding of these scientific findings and shape our social and ethical choices in the years ahead.

...what degree of mediation is appropriate to ensure that the art—particularly challenging conceptual art—will effectively stimulate civic dialogue?

What Degree of Mediation Between the Artist and Viewer is Appropriate? What Constitutes Civic Dialogue?

The *Gene(sis)* project stretched the Henry to consider ways to engage audiences in civic dialogue and, in doing so, raised key questions about arts-based dialogue concepts and practices. For the Henry curators, the intent of civic dialogue often appeared to be at odds with their goal of allowing the artwork to "speak for itself," at times creating tension regarding whether the dialogue was driving the art. That tension manifested itself in the Henry's approach to the interpretation of the *Gene(sis)* artwork, which stressed the museum's curatorial/educational viewpoint that the work be presented in an unobtrusive, neutral way in order to encourage unmediated dialogue between the artist and viewer. The Henry staff saw this approach as a way of empowering audiences to draw their own conclusions about the provocative issues raised by the artists.

The Henry's approach stood in stark contrast to other museum-based Lab projects that presented artwork dealing with difficult and controversial subject matter. At the other end of the spectrum was The Jewish Museum's approach to its presentation of *Mirroring Evil: Nazi Imagery/Recent Art*, which maximized contextualization of the artwork for audiences. In doing so, The Jewish Museum staff posited a different curatorial/educational perspective: an abundance of contextual materials would promote, rather than inhibit, dialogue among viewers. These divergent approaches raise a central question about arts-based dialogue practice relevant to all Lab participants: what degree of mediation is appropriate to ensure that the art—particularly challenging conceptual art—will effectively stimulate civic dialogue? While Lab participants were divided on this question, the consensus seemed to be that, particularly with regard to artwork that has the potential to be controversial and/or polarizing, too much information rather than too little would better serve the goal of promoting dialogue and mitigating the potential for misunderstanding.

What Constitutes Civic Dialogue?

Deliberations about the appropriate level of mediation led Seattle participants to ponder the larger question of how art functions as "dialogue" between artist and viewer. Does the "interchange of ideas" between the artist and viewer through an artwork constitute civic dialogue? In this respect, the Henry's explorations of viewer experience and response to the *Gene(sis)* artwork shed a light on the "dialogue with self" that is inherent in experiencing art and grappling with the ideas the artwork evokes. While dialogue is generally defined as an exchange of ideas and opinions between two or more persons, does it necessarily need to be a collective experience? And what is the place of "dialogue with self" in relation to civic dialogue? As the Henry staff put forth through the *Gene(sis)* project, "dialogue with self" may well be part of the continuum toward civic dialogue.

Artistic and Dialogic Outcomes

In view of the *Gene(sis)* project's primary artistic intent—to organize a major touring exhibition that would elucidate and provoke dialogue about new developments in human genome research—it was highly successful on many levels. The exhibition was of high artistic merit and critically well-received. It generated significant local and national media attention, with coverage in major newspapers as well as in leading cultural and scientific journals and magazines. *Gene(sis)* was even the subject of a feature article in the the *New York Times* Arts and Leisure section on May 26, 2002.

Gene(sis) was also successful in its intent to serve as an entry point for lay audiences into highly technical materials with potentially profound social implications. Its four themes—SEQUENCE, BOUNDARY, SPECIMAN, and SUBJECT—provided the viewer with a useful framework for understanding and exploring the artwork in relation to the scientific findings to which the artist was responding. While audiences may have found some pieces less accessible than others, and a few decidedly disturbing, all the artwork provoked viewers to consider genomic research. As one viewer commented, "Whether this exhibit touches your 'spooky' nerve, or your aesthetic sensibility, or your logician's cortex, there is bound to be a piece here that provokes you."

In terms of dialogic outcomes, the *Gene(sis)* project was particularly effective in its engagement of a large portion of the Seattle community in considering the significance of human genome research as an important topic of public conversation. Judging by attendance at the *Gene(sis)* premiere—1,200 people attended the opening, and the symposium on the opening weekend was sold out—the project captured the interest of local residents and, through the exhibition and public programs, provided a civic "space" for further learning and dialogue about these issues.

"Whether this exhibit touches your 'spooky' nerve, or your aesthetic sensibility, or your logician's cortex, there is bound to be a piece here that provokes you."

In design and implementation, the public programs, like the exhibition itself, offered the community multiple entry points into the topic of human genome research. The variety of programming—facilitated book readings, author talks, film screenings, academic gatherings, and creative writing courses, as well as the symposium and public meetings—appealed to diverse audiences, such as academics, students, writers, policymakers, and the general public. The Henry's conscious integration of structured dialogue elements in selected programs provided the opportunity for dialogue among participants. Through the Genetics Task Force Public Meeting the Henry also attempted to link art to public deliberations shaping policymaking around genetic research.

Another significant outcome was the number of valuable products developed in conjunction with the *Gene(sis)* project. The Henry's educational staff developed an exemplary 65-page curriculum guide with appendices for use by teachers in the classroom and in conjunction with school visits to the exhibition. This interdisciplinary guide—with 19 slides containing background information on *Gene(sis)* artists and artwork, discussion questions, a glossary, and a bibliography—prepares teachers to tackle the subject of art and genomics. The guide was made available to public school teachers in the Puget Sound region and to a consortium of member museums of the American Association of Museums.

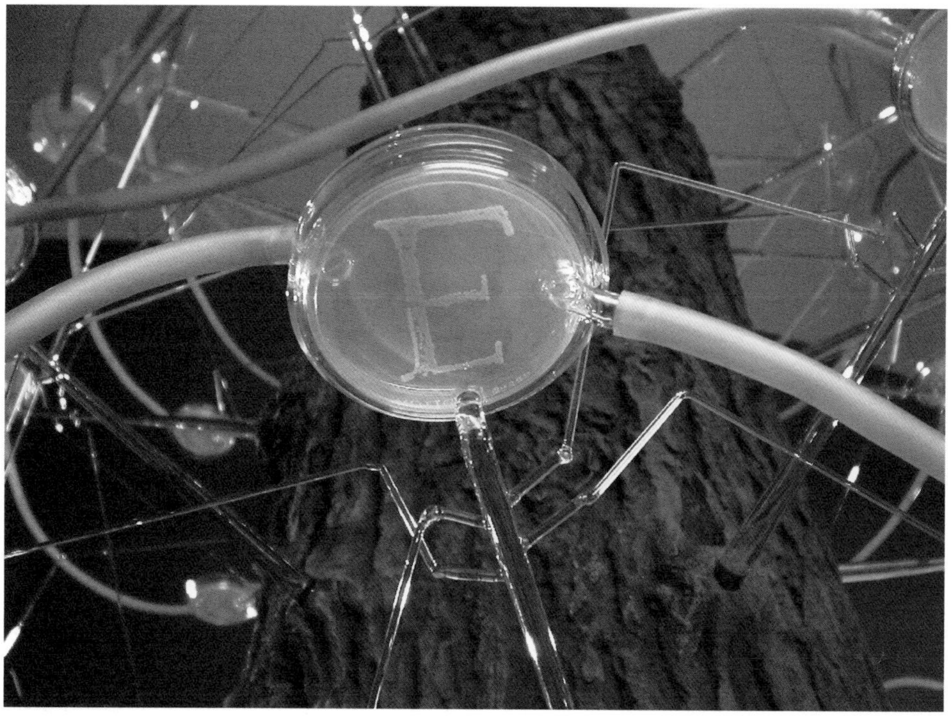

Jill Reynolds, Family Tree II *(detail), 2002.*
Courtesy of the artist.

In lieu of a printed catalogue, the Henry created an accessible, well-designed CD-ROM exhibition catalogue that enables the user to view the *Gene(sis)* artwork in a three-dimensional, interactive manner. In addition to artist biographies, critical essays, and information resources, the CD-ROM also includes video clips of performances by the Critical Art Ensemble and artists interviews. The *Gene(sis)* website, designed as an online companion to the exhibition and multilayered resource center, is available on the Internet. It is being used regularly as a valuable record of the exhibition and its themes, as well as a resource for current issues, such as the investigation of CAE artist Steve Kurtz's artistic practices and use of biological materials. As *Gene(sis)* traveled from museum to museum, the website was tailored to each host's configuration and local needs and concerns. A toolbox was created to document the extensive programs and provide background on the artists and artworks, as well as the wall texts. It also served to assist tour site organizers in developing their own arts-based civic dialogue programs.

Given the project's ambitious size and scope, there were inevitably a number of missed opportunities. While the Henry and the *Gene(sis)* working group conceptualized a compelling framework for the public programs component—"Paradigms Lost and Found," "Designer Bodies," "Bioethics and Public Policy," "Public Conceptions and Misperceptions about Human Genomics" and "The Concept of Aesthetic Elegance in Art and Science"—these five "Public Programs Issues" were not explicitly linked to the actual programming, nor were they explored with the depth and rigor that might have been possible. Another opportunity not fully explored was the dialogue that occurred between the artists and scientists who collaborated on the three works commissioned by the Henry for the

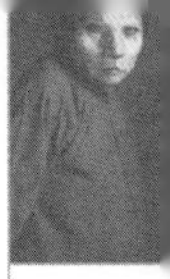

exhibition. In view of the Henry's artistic interest in exploring the intersection of fine art and hard science, documenting the dialogue between artists and scientists may well have illuminated these junctures in new ways and shed light on the dialogic process by which the artwork was created. Finally, while the Henry invested significant resources in the development of a logic model and evaluative tools to measure audience response, no one has analyzed the data. If evaluated in some meaningful way, the data could indicate which dialogue formats were successful, the ways in which audiences interacted with and responded to the exhibit and public programs, and the impact that project activities had on public awareness and understanding of the issues *Gene(sis)* raised.

Overall, the *Gene(sis)* project heightened public awareness about human genome research and, through the scope of its communitywide public programming, offered multiple ways for the Seattle community to engage in these issues. Because of national media attention and the U.S. tour, the exhibition's impact continues to ripple through communities beyond Puget Sound. The *Gene(sis)* project also underscores the role that contemporary art can play in drawing public attention to human genome research as a civic issue in a uniquely compelling way, and in contributing to a richer and broader understanding and discussion of the complex ideas surrounding biogenetics.

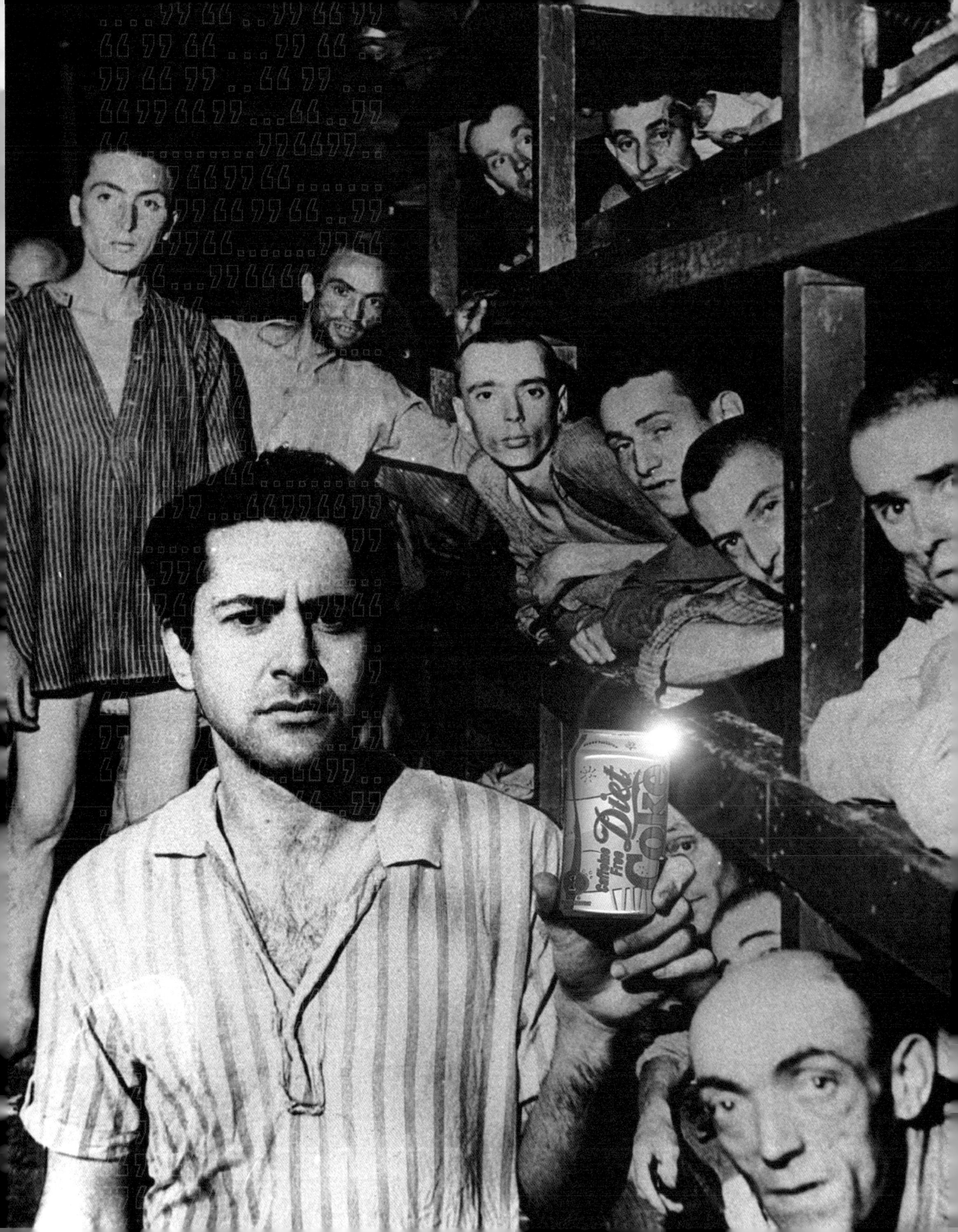
Caffeine Free
Diet
Coke

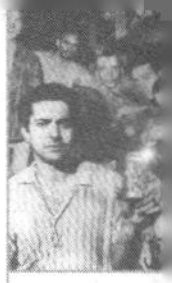

2 The Jewish Museum

::: *MIRRORING EVIL: NAZI IMAGERY/RECENT ART*

JEANNE PEARLMAN

PREFACE

This case study describes the artistic and dialogic intents and outcomes of *Mirroring Evil: Nazi Imagery/Recent Art* (March 13 through June 30, 2002), an exhibition organized by The Jewish Museum, an art museum located in New York City.

The intent of The Jewish Museum in organizing this exhibition is best captured in a statement that describes the institution's belief that *Mirroring Evil* would function as a:

Alan Schechner, Self Portrait at Buchenwald: It's the Real Thing. *1991–1993. Courtesy of the artist.*

> ...springboard for dialogue about the complicity and complacency toward evil in today's society. The museum will show work by...artists who have eschewed the deeply entrenched Holocaust imagery that focuses on the victim. Instead, they use images of perpetrators—Nazis—to provoke viewers to explore the culture of victimhood...[1]

This case study will contend that the exhibition, combined with The Jewish Museum's laudable interest in facilitating dialogue on a complex and difficult subject, made it the ideal site for arts-based civic dialogue. In an era of declining attendance and support for art museums in this country, the successes and challenges experienced by the museum

[1] This case drew substantially upon reports by The Jewish Museum to Animating Democracy.

can serve as a learning opportunity for those cultural institutions that seek to expand their engagement with the public beyond the normal public programming model of expert panels and interpretative materials.

Mirroring Evil included 19 works by 13 younger artists who examine the representation of National Socialist images by mass culture, interpreted through the consciousness of a generation that had not even been born when the events of the Holocaust unfolded. It is certainly not new for artists to explore the notion of evil through the lens of the Holocaust. What is unusual is to situate their exploration within the context of imagery that attempts to explore the forbidden character of the perpetrator. Holocaust art has been confined, in most cases, to the memorialization and sacralization of the victims and their stories. *Mirroring Evil* offered artists, only four of whom are Jewish, the opportunity to shift the perspective and examine the perpetrators as a means to identify the distinguishing characteristics of evil. The result, as is often the case when the ground beneath our feet begins to shift, could be dizzying.

It is certainly not new for artists to explore the notion of evil through the lens of the Holocaust. What is unusual is to situate their exploration within the context of imagery that attempts to explore the forbidden character of the perpetrator.

This case study will examine several features of this project: the institutions and individuals involved, the planning process from curatorial intent to exhibition design to dialogic opportunities, brief descriptions of the artwork, the nature and effects of the arts-based civic dialogue, and finally an analysis of the public reception and the controversy that erupted before the exhibition ever opened its doors.

THE PARTICIPANTS

The Jewish Museum was founded in 1904, with a gift of 26 Jewish ceremonial artworks by Judge Mayer Sulzberger to The Jewish Theological Seminary. The museum continues to use its collection to explore Jewish culture and over the years has taken its place among the major cultural institutions of New York. The Jewish Museum reaches out to diverse populations, within and outside of the Jewish community, through a collection of more than 28,000 objects, including paintings and sculptures, works on paper, photographs, archaeological artifacts, ceremonial objects, and broadcast media. It is also committed to public programming that serves as both audience development and cultural outreach. Since 1957, the museum has been located at Fifth Avenue and 92nd Street, along New York's prestigious Museum Mile. In 1993, an ambitious expansion increased the gallery space and permanent exhibition spaces, and added classrooms and an auditorium for educational programs.

Norman Kleeblatt, The Jewish Museum's Susan and Elihu Rose Curator of Fine Arts, has been a curator at the museum since 1981. During the last 20 years, he has played a major role in the direction of the museum's exhibition program and the development of its collection of modern and contemporary art. In his work as a curator, Kleeblatt has never been wary of investigating a topic that is seen as taboo. He curated *The Dreyfus Affair: Art, Truth and Justice* (1987), an exhibition that presented visual art produced in France at the end of the 19th century during the time of the trial and imprisonment of Alfred Dreyfus, a Jewish military officer who was falsely accused of treason. The virulent anti-Semitism of that time was reflected in the material shown in the exhibition. Yet Kleeblatt was not seeking to shock Jewish audiences. Rather, he was intrigued with the role that artists had

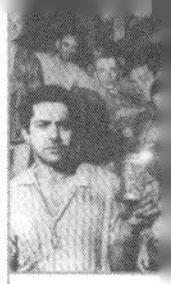

played in supporting the perpetrators of the affair, as well as in some cases Dreyfus's defenders. Kleeblatt used the historical artwork to examine the role of the media in documenting as well as in fermenting the crisis. He writes:

> The Affair established for the first time in history a new role of social and political activism for writers, artists, and academicians, setting the pace for the involvement of the same groups in the ever more pressing and harrowing dilemmas of the twentieth century... This was an era that thrived on information (the more skewed and sensational, the better) and materialism (which grew ever more commercialized and accessible). And it frequently fused and confused these two.[2]

In 1991, Kleeblatt turned to an exploration of Jewish identity in the exhibition, *Too Jewish? Challenging Traditional Identities*. This exhibition explored the question of when, where, and how Jewish artists would choose—or perhaps be invited—to participate in the postmodern discourse on identity-based representation. The exhibition invited 23 young Jewish artists to:

> ...recast their Jewish past in the matrix of postwar America, including both positive and negative aspects of growing up as a white *Other* in what was formerly seen as the munificent melting pot. Few pay attention to earlier Jewish pasts—the shtetls and ghettos of Europe or New York's Lower East Side, places about which previous generations still wax nostalgic. And the Holocaust, which occupies a central position within the construction of contemporary Jewish identity, is addressed ambivalently or critically, if it is addressed at all.[3]

These two exhibitions reflected Kleeblatt's belief that The Jewish Museum should present work that addresses timely and often difficult social issues. His commitment to the open discussion of even controversial social issues is further represented in *Mirroring Evil*.

The Jewish Museum Staff is an outstanding team of museum professionals who worked with Kleeblatt in conceptualizing and implementing both the exhibition and the accompanying public programming. Working with Kleeblatt as part of the curatorial team was Joanna Lindenbaum, assistant curator of the exhibition. Lindenbaum and Kleeblatt worked closely together, with the latter serving both as mentor and colleague to his younger counterpart. Lindenbaum should be credited for her willingness to conceive new ways of collaborating with other departments and particularly in forging a collegial dynamic with her counterparts in the education department. From the outset, the team was determined to forge a new model of how a museum could work with this challenging material and to fully integrate the public programming within the curatorial plan. They began by including Carole Zawatsky, the director of education, as a critical member of the team. Ignoring what can be an impenetrable hierarchy within museums, curatorial, educational, and public programming staff worked together to assure a seamless plan to accomplish the common goal of exhibiting, contextualizing, and interpreting the artworks. While there were occasional clashes, The Jewish Museum developed an interdepartmental model that was predicated on mutual respect and a commitment to internal dialogue. This new way of working represented a significant accomplishment of the project, which staff believe will continue in the future.[4]

[2] Norman Kleeblatt, "The Dreyfus Affair: A Visual Record."

[3] Norman Kleeblatt, "Passing Into Multiculturalism," in *Too Jewish? Challenging Traditional Identities*, 7.

[4] In a conversation with Lindenbaum in November 2003, she reports that the dialogic and collaborative model established during *Mirroring Evil* continues to work well on subsequent projects. She commented that since *Mirroring Evil*, the entire staff recognizes that education is not about classes for children, but rather about integrating educational and interpretive materials throughout the planning for every exhibition.

In addition to Kleeblatt, Lindenbaum, and Zawatsky, the museum team involved in the project included Ruth Beesch, deputy director for programs, and Ann Scher, director of communication, as well as many other members of the staff who were involved at various stages of the planning. Museum Director Joan Rosenbaum was frequently involved and played an important role in supporting and communicating the curatorial vision to trustees and others in the community.

The Collaborators comprised institutions that were selected based upon the museum's interest in developing programming for adults, school groups, and educators, and to provide opportunities to involve others within the city of New York in the process of framing the civic issues inherent within and tangential to the exhibition. In particular, the museum reports that The National Center for Jewish Learning and Leadership played a key role in defining those issues that might arise within the very diverse Jewish community as well as other potential audiences who would be drawn into dialogue through the artists' work. The collaborators and their contributions included:

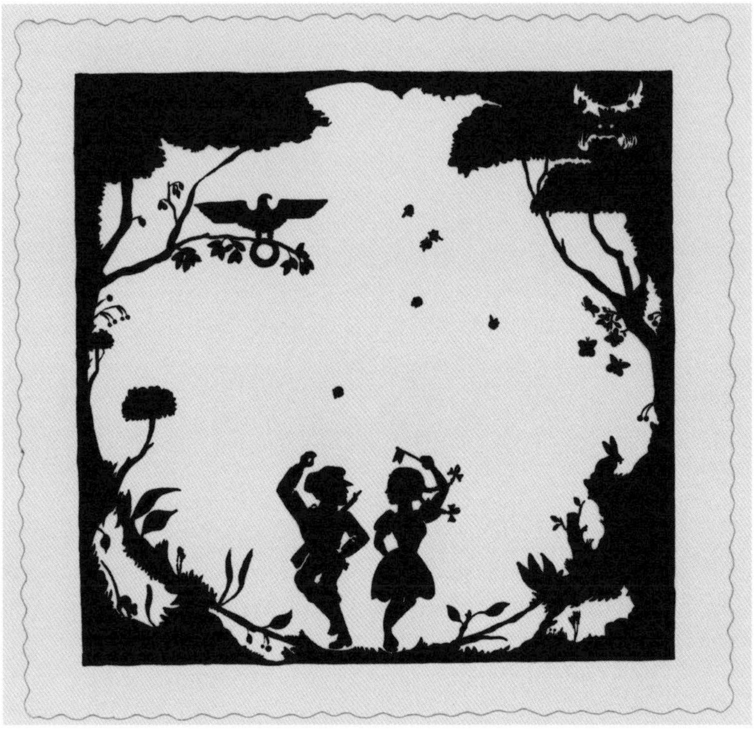

Roee Rosen, Live and Die as Eva Braun *#34 (detail). 1995. Courtesy of the artist.*

The National Jewish Center for Learning and Leadership (CLAL) is a think tank, leadership training institute, and resource center whose activities are dedicated to building a Jewish life that is spiritually vibrant and engaged with the intellectual and ethical challenges of the wider world. CLAL's faculty represents an unusual mix of rabbis from every denomination and scholars from an array of disciplines. Working with established and emerging volunteer leaders, rabbis, and Jewish professionals, CLAL has earned a reputation for provocative programming that embodies the principles of pluralism and helps to revitalize institutions. The Jewish Museum staff report that CLAL played a key role in the framing of issues for *Mirroring Evil*. The museum team met with CLAL staff regularly to discuss issues pertinent to the exhibition and this engagement was seen as particularly helpful in framing approaches to engaging both Jewish and non-Jewish communities.

Facing History and Ourselves engages students of diverse backgrounds in citizenship education. Civic education encourages the skills, promotes the values, and fosters the ideals needed to sustain a democratic society. Peter Nelson from Facing History and Ourselves worked with Michelle Asche, the museum manager for school and outreach, to provide advice and comments regarding the educator guide. Nelson also participated in the planning for the teacher workshops.

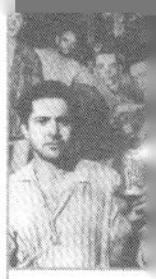

The Vera List Center for Art and Politics at The New School, founded in 1992 with the generous support of philanthropist Vera List, is the university's vehicle for debate, discussion, research, and reflection concerning the complex and vital relationship between politics and the arts. Committed to ensuring the future of democratic culture, the Center serves as a forum for those seeking an open analysis of relevant issues. Toward this end, the Center develops public lectures, courses, symposia, publications, research activities, and focused study groups. The Center collaborated with the museum to organize a panel and a dialogue related to the *Mirroring Evil* exhibition and provided advisory support on the whole of the project. These programs were held under the aegis of New School University, formerly the New School for Social Research, established in 1917 by a group of New York City intellectuals and committed to and organized around principles of social and political change.

The Humanities and Social Sciences Library of The New York Public Library encourages the preservation and cultivation of the documentary evidence of human behavior, social life, and culture, by acquiring, organizing, and making accessible materials for study in the fields of history, languages and literature, art, popular culture, philosophy, religion, psychology, sociology, anthropology, theology, geography, and politics. In conjunction with *Mirroring Evil*, the library presented a lecture about anti-Semitism and music.

PLANNING ACTIVITIES

From the beginning, the goal was to organize an exhibition of contemporary art and an accompanying catalogue to stimulate dialogue around the issues raised by the artists in their work. Within this approach, it became necessary to design a series of extensive educational and public programming components in order to deal with the underlying issues the project might raise. It was also considered important that the overall project include interpretative materials to deal not only with the wide variety of media being used by the artists but also to address content issues in a way that served as outreach to the museum's multiple audiences. These interpretive materials included:

- two videos commissioned to contextualize the work in an aesthetic and historical frame of reference;
- a series of text panels, labels, and artists' statements; and
- an exhibition catalogue.

Inclusive Planning

Different from past exhibitions, the education department collaborated with the curatorial department to interpret the issues and ideas of the works of art and the exhibition as a whole. The engagement among the core staff and other departments of the museum was extremely helpful in formulating the planning process. In a thoughtful and insightful final report, the museum notes that the exhibition provided the opportunity to design and implement an innovative methodology for the institution's departments to work together toward a common goal.

> Responsibilities and functions within the institution shifted during the course of the *Mirroring Evil* project. Each and every department of the museum participated in the

> planning or implementation... Throughout the planning stages, the curatorial team worked much more closely with the education, public programming, and public relations departments of the museum than for past exhibitions.

After more than three years of planning, several civic issues were identified as arising both from the collective conceptual framework of the exhibition and from the individual artists' work. The process itself was described as highly dialogic, and the museum reported that the project evolved and transformed, changing and improving time and again.

This commitment to an inclusive and collaborative process served the museum well, not only in its success in developing the exhibition and its interpretive materials but also in forming a cohesive team that was broadly representative of the institution.

Ultimately, after much discussion and debate, the following issues were stated as the core questions of the exhibition and its public programming:

- **Who can speak for the Holocaust?** Can only survivors speak? How can subsequent generations gain understanding and apply the lessons of the past?

- **How has art used Nazi imagery to represent evil?** What happens to our understanding of history as film, television, and other art forms convert the Nazis into symbols?

- **What are the limits of irreverence?** To what extent may artists overstep the bounds of taste, in confronting facts that are outrageous and terrifying? Do some art forms work against themselves?

- **Why must we confront evil?** What are the dangers of ignoring the past or being complacent about the present?

- **How has art helped to break the silence?** When reality seems to be unspeakable, how may art open a dialogue and keep memory alive?

...each question was designed to promote dialogue rather than shut it down. This value was apparent throughout the museum's public programming.

The individuals who worked to frame these questions did so from a point of view that reflected the underlying core values of the project. First, each question was designed to promote dialogue rather than shut it down. This value was apparent throughout the museum's public programming. Second, while the questions were designed to be as straightforward as possible, they were also intended to touch on many other civic issues inherent to the project. According to the museum's interim report to Animating Democracy:

> ...For example, the question, "Who can speak for the Holocaust?," raises the issue of relativization of the Jewish Holocaust and what can be learned in terms of other Holocausts. And the question, "Why must we confront evil?," raises questions of victimhood within the Jewish communities as well as in other minority communities.

The staff recognized that the evolving dialogue that led to the formulation of these questions resulted in a deeper understanding of the issues on the part of the artists and staff

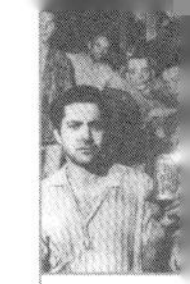

as well as the various collaborators, advisors, and partners. From July to November 2000, Kleeblatt and Lindenbaum convened various community leaders to advise and assist with the development of the interpretive strategies and to aid the construction of civic dialogues. Zawatsky played an important role in designing and implementing these meetings. She envisioned these gatherings as a resource to elicit feedback on potential community responses to the exhibition. Participants included museum and other educators as well as lay leaders from the Jewish community and those involved in the study of the Holocaust. Throughout their deliberations, the various committees consciously employed a dialogic model in their discussions. The advisory committees examined the exhibition's imagery and its multiple associations and interpretations. All the responses and feedback were evaluated and taken into careful consideration during the planning stages, and several were incorporated as major components of the projects. The advisory groups were divided into three distinct populations, and their comments were instrumental in the museum's design of the exhibition and the interpretative materials that accompanied it.

The advisory committees examined the exhibition's imagery and its multiple associations and interpretations.

The following groups met with museum staff in the above mentioned ways to provide advice and feedback in the development of *Mirroring Evil* and around issues and needs that came up during its run.

Scholar Meetings. Kleeblatt notes that scholar's meetings are often used for complex exhibitions organized by the museum. In this case, the discussions focused on:

> ...the meaning and history of art and literature related to the Holocaust, the primacy of memory culture, and the urge of these artists—reflected also in the writings of a number of academics and critics—to move beyond the reverential. There were also those who considered an urgent need to find some relevance for teaching about World War II and the Holocaust in light of the tragedies and violence that continue to take place today.

Board of Director Meetings. Staff report that the members of The Jewish Museum board played a vital role in preparing for the exhibition. Staff met collectively, and in many cases individually, with board members to review the conceptual framework for the exhibition, to familiarize them with individual works of art, and to assure that they would be well prepared to field questions and concerns from donors, members, and others in the community. Moreover, many trustees provided input on the project's issues, the interpretive methods, public programs, as well as actively supported public outreach by bringing visitors to the museum.

Community Advisory and Advisory Board Meetings. Prior to the opening of the exhibition, Zawatsky met with approximately 20 individuals including survivors, scholars, religious leaders, and children of survivors to review the images, as well as their associations and interpretations, and to discuss the issues relevant to the exhibition. All feedback and ideas exchanged in these meetings were taken into careful consideration during the planning stages of the project. Regarding the input of the advisory board, the staff note that this group played an instrumental role in the idea to produce a "talking heads" video that would capture the diverse points of view regarding issues explored in the exhibition. Zawatsky writes that "...this video would pave a way for our visitors to experience, to a degree, the spirit and dynamics of the conversations that had taken place in more intimate settings.

In addition, the museum believed that an introductory video was necessary to set the stage for what visitors might expect to see within the exhibition. In comments captured for the interim report, Maurice Berger, a nationally recognized cultural critic, shared his vision for the introductory video:

> I was asked to produce a video that would help set some of the exhibition's central issues in a social and cultural context. I realized that the content of the exhibition was controversial in nature and suggested creating a video that would remind viewers that many of the exhibition's central issues—the nature of the Holocaust and Nazism and the seduction and repulsion of violence and evil—have long been examined by the culture at large... The five-minute video I produced contains clips from popular films and television programs of the past 50 years—fragments from popular culture that ask us to reflect upon our own relationship to the central questions and issues of the exhibition...

Based on advisor meetings, the museum decided not to produce an exhibition audio guide and not to make the website a major component of the dialogue. Listening to an audio guide might distract from dialogue and original thought within the galleries. Instead of engaging in the works of art, the public would be passive rather then actively involved. Staff decided not to host public dialogues on the museum's website due to the excess of misinformation about the project that circulated in and out of the press prior to the opening of the exhibition.

Junior Staff Dialogue Meetings. Lindenbaum convened meetings to capture the responses of a younger generation, born in the 1970s and 1980s. It is interesting to note that all of the participating artists were at least one generation removed from the Holocaust and under 38 years of age. Lindenbaum reported on the museum's interest in engaging in dialogue with younger people, and this effort began with the junior staff, defined as those under the age of 32. The outcomes of the dialogue reflected its diversity, from religious to nonobservant, and from grandchildren of Holocaust survivors to Germans, African Americans, and others. There was no unanimity of point of view, although the works in the exhibition disturbed many of the members of the younger group. Lindenbaum reports:

> Contrary to what we had expected, many members of this younger group were very disturbed by the works and the subject matter. A heated discussion developed about whether or not it was appropriate for the artists to single out specific consumer brands and about whether the group's Jewish participants should respond differently from non-Jewish participants to the issues at hand.

This dialogue resulted in a major constructive idea, one that impacted the overall organization of the exhibition: this group preferred to be asked questions within an exhibition as opposed to being given close-ended information.

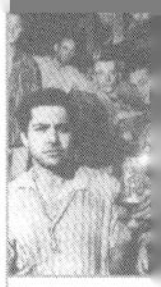

In each case, the museum staff report that these engagements with various segments in the community were critical to their work. Kleeblatt used his scholar meetings to stimulate his thinking and initially to identify participants who might make a contribution to the catalogue. Zawatsky writes that dialogue with the community strengthened her own convictions regarding the importance of the exhibition. Both Zawatsky and Lindenbaum note that concrete suggestions made by various outside groups were later incorporated into the design of the exhibition.

Curatorial Intent

In his catalogue essay, Kleeblatt begins with a discussion of the transgressive nature of the work of Anselm Kiefer, a German artist whose paintings consistently utilize iconic images from Germany's national socialist past. Kleeblatt draws upon the work of cultural theorist Andreas Huyssen, whose analysis of Kiefer's work offers a possible rationale for why this post-war artist continues to navigate the treacherous boundaries of the taboo in reminding Germans of a past they'd rather forget.

> The issue...is not whether to forget or to remember, but rather how to remember and how to handle representations of the remembered past at a time when most of us...only know that past through images, films, photographs, and representations... To say it in yet another way, Kiefer's haunted images...do not challenge the representations of those who refuse to face the terror of the past; rather they challenge the repressions of those who do remember and who do accept the burden of fascism on German national identity.[5]

[5] Andreas Huyssen, "Anselm Kiefer: The Terror of History, the Temptation of Myth," in *Twilight Memories: Marking Time in a Culture of Amnesia* (New York: Routledge, 1995), 215.

Kleeblatt's catalogue essay is significant in giving evidence to his interest in the role of art in demystifying the realm of the forbidden and taboo, particularly as it pertains to how those taboos form Jewish identity. He is most eloquent, however, when he describes the paradox inherent in the early work of Boris Lurie, a Russian-born Buchenwald survivor. In a series of large-scale collages, *Saturation Paintings–1959–64,* Lurie both entices and repels

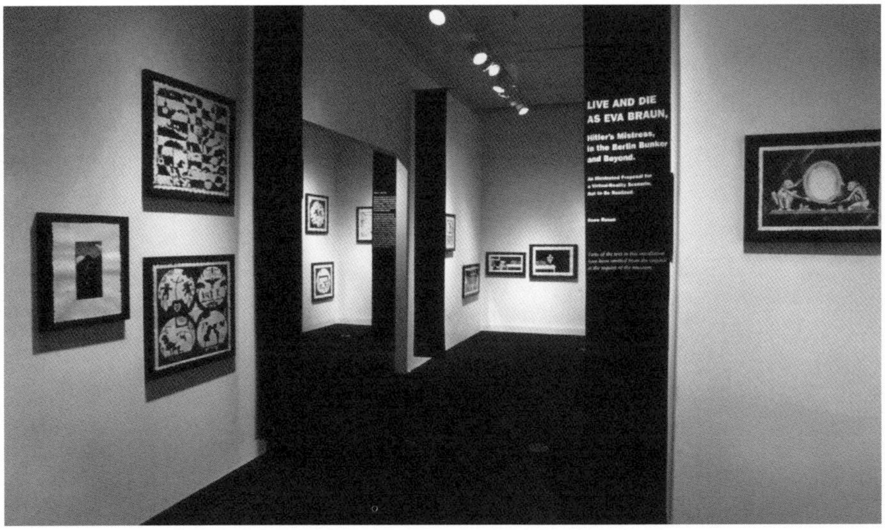

View of installation of Live and Die as Eva Braun, *Roee Rosen, 1995. Photo by David Heald.*

the viewer's gaze through the conflation of images of emaciated survivors and licentious pinups of the same era. Like the Lustmörd paintings of Weimar Germany, Lurie's work taunts the viewer with its voyeuristic seduction, the forbidden glimpses into the basest landscape of the human soul. Kleeblatt wonders why these images continue to shock even after the far more sexually graphic work of Mapplethorpe or the religious transgression of Serrano would seem to have desensitized our collective capacity for outrage. He reflects on the question of transgression and art:

> Lurie collages crossed boundaries. But who sets these boundaries, and who dares to traverse them? Not least, who has a right to?[6]

[6] Norman Kleeblatt, "Passing Into Multiculturalism," in *Too Jewish? Challenging Traditional Identities*, 11.

The underlying spirit expressed in the question, "Who has the right?," is repeated in one of the core questions of the exhibition, namely, "Who owns the Holocaust?" Kleeblatt's answer is the essence of this exhibition. He selected the work of artists who:

> ...use Nazi imagery—the ultimate signifier of evil—to mirror moral and ethical issues that resonate in contemporary society. Each artist puts the viewer in the uncomfortable terrain between good and evil, seduction and repulsion... They surround viewers with the unmentionable, bring them close to synecdoches for evil, then leave them to ponder the inexorable complexity of ethics.[7]

[7] Ibid.

Kleeblatt was prescient in his understanding that positioning the viewer in the terrain between good and evil, surrounded by icons of the unmentionable, often leaves him or her free to actualize the work through the lens of an individualized and eccentric definition of transgression and taboo. Hence, every depiction of evil is a potential assault and every incursion through the boundary into the realm of the forbidden must be punished. Such was often the case with the reception and response to *Mirroring Evil*, and a critical question for consideration is whether the museum's ensuing steps toward mediating and interpreting the works as well as design of the dialogic program was successful in its adherence to the curatorial vision and intent while attempting to ameliorate the genuine pain and sense of betrayal experienced by some constituents.

The Artists

Mirroring Evil includes 19 works by 13 artists, four of whom are Jewish.

Boaz Arad (born 1956), Israel. "Hebrew Lessons" (2000) splices together segments of film and sound bites from some of Hitler's public speeches, ending with a video of Hitler saying "Shalom Yerushalayim, ani mitnatzel," Hebrew for "Hello Jerusalem, I apologize."

Christine Borland (born 1965), Scotland. "L'Homme Double: Keeping One's Hands Clean: Six Commissioned Portraits of a Perpetrator" consists of six plaster busts of Nazi doctor Joseph Mengele, created by six forensic sculptors who worked from blurry photographs and descriptions given to them by the artist.

Rudolf Herz (born 1954), Germany. "Zugzwang" (1995) consists of a 1932 portrait of Hitler and a 1912 portrait of Marcel Duchamp, both created by Hitler's official portrait photographer, Heinrich Hoffmann. Herz wallpapered one room of the gallery with these

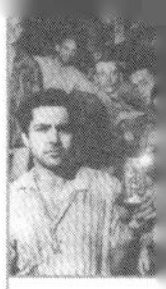

images, repeated like a checkerboard. The title is a chess term describing apposition in which any possible move will make the situation worse. The viewer is asked to look at these two iconic figures, the dictator and the Dadaist as interpreted and homogenized by the lens of the camera.

Matt Kollishaw (born 1955), England. "Burnt Almonds: Gustav & Helga" feature two reticular light-box photos showing Nazi officers and half-dressed women in a theatrical recreation of Hitler's suicide bunker.

Elke Krystufek (born 1970), Vienna. "Economical Live" is made up of elements of Nazi and contemporary nude images collaged into a large-scale painting.

Misha Kubball (born 1958), Germany. "Hitler's Cabinet" consists of a large plywood cross. From the end of each wooden beam, lighted projections of German film stills are cast onto the floor, creating the overall image of a swastika.

Zbigniew Libera (born 1959), Poland. "LEGO Concentration Camp Set" is a set of seven boxes with the familiar toy company logo floating above images for an imaginary toy concentration camp.

Roee Rosen (born 1963), Israel. "Live and Die as Eva Braun" (1995) seeks to depict the final moments in the infamous Hitler-mistress's life, complete with her premonition of descending to hell.

Tom Sachs (born 1966), United States. "Giftgas Giftset" (1998) consists of "designer" Xyklon B gas cans decorated with Chanel, Hermès, and Tiffany & Co. logos.

The entire planning and design processes were punctuated by a series of town meeting-type forums, each of which included dissenting as well as encouraging voices from diverse fields.

Allen Schechner (born 1962), England. "Self-Portrait at Buchenwald: It's the Real Thing" is a Web-based work that inserts the artist into a Margaret Bourke-White photograph of Jewish inmates in Buchenwald. He's standing in front of them, dressed as they are but looking well and healthy and holding a can of Diet Coke.

Alain Séchas (born 1955), France. "Enfants Gâtes" includes four perfectly aligned posts upon which sit toy cats, with Hitler hairstyles and mustaches and swastika baby rattles. One is surrounded by mirrors to the left and right, creating the illusion of an infinite army of Hitler cats.

Maciej Toporowicz (born 1958), Poland. "Eternity #14" places Nazi imagery of perfection and the body next to reproduction of these same images in Calvin Klein advertisements.

Piotr Uklański (born 1968), Poland. "The Nazis" (1998) compiles 147 photographs and illustrations of actors portraying Nazis in films, including virtually every major Hollywood figure of the past 50 years.

Exhibition Design

The museum team worked with two separate consultants to design the exhibition: architect Dan Kershaw and architectural artist Allan Wexler. The intent was to produce a design that

ARTIST INVOLVEMENT IN EXHIBITION PLANNING AND PROGRAMS

"Planning *Mirroring Evil* also affected the institution in its approach to working with artists. Because of the difficult, sensitive, and controversial nature of the project, those artists invited to show in *Mirroring Evil* were much more involved in this exhibition than in others. Their increased participation is due in part to Animating Democracy, which required three artist letters of commitment for the grant application. This prompted the museum to involve some of the artists very early on in the interpretation of the exhibition, as well as the ideas of civic dialogue and exchange between diverse participants. Each of the artists was brought to New York for preparatory round table discussions prior to the exhibition, and to participate in the interviews of the talking heads video. Their ideas and suggestions were taken into consideration in the exhibition planning, its interpretive components, and surrounding programs. The museum staff hope the meeting, the exhibition, and all *Mirroring Evil* programs have created an impact on the artists and their practices. Going forward, the museum anticipates using the relationship with artists as a model, and to incorporate and consult with artists in its future projects. The museum has gained the understanding that it is essential to incorporate artists' ideas, backgrounds, and thoughts into its exhibitions. In addition, *Mirroring Evil* became an important experience for the artists."

—Joanna Lindenbaum, associate curator

"One critical comment that more than one art pro made was that the textual and pedagogical apparatus surrounding *Mirroring Evil* was excessive, interfering with the work, and seemed overly defensive. While I could identify on a personal level with this sentiment, the passionate (and often aggressive) reactions to the exhibition provided ample proof that this apparatus was justified. Not only were the issues charged enough to have many outraged voices prior to the opening, but more importantly the discursive ambitions of Curator Norman Kleeblatt were remarkable in the courage to tackle complicated and volatile issues—and to do so in a way that engaged a wide array of individuals as well as making it tangible to the strictly art public. In this sense, I believe the show was an all too rare demonstration of art's capacity to transcend its elitist (and often insular and obfuscated) realm, and do so without compromising its complexity and integrity. This extraordinary success, I believe, resulted in an intense engagement of so many—from holocaust survivors to art critics—in the dialogue, and also in a long-term process of thought, experience, and conversation that continues still, and will continue long after the exhibition closes."

—Roee Rosen, Mirroring Evil *artist*

"Participating in the exhibition, *Mirroring Evil*, was a unique and stimulating experience for me. The premise behind the exhibition was brave, exciting, and inventive, and, in addition, the input and support of Animating Democracy allowed a range of different kinds of dialogue to emerge. Many of these dialogues are, to say the least, uncommon within the traditional format of a group show. Most unique was the opportunity to meet with and engage in dialogues with my fellow artists in the exhibition. This is the first time I have been involved in a meeting of this nature, and it allowed introducing both the artists and their ideas. Very often, in the process of curating and criticism, the artist's voice is lost in the interpretations of others. Being able to hear first-hand from the artists provided everyone with a deeper and more informed understanding of the exhibition's works. In addition, the meeting also included the museum representatives and those of the funding agencies, many of whom under normal circumstances would not have direct contact with artists prior to the show.

I know that the show was attacked by some in the art world as over-contextualizing the art and ideas behind the show; however I believe this to be not just false, but elitist. It is a product of those in the art world who do not want work that deals with real issues and are also not interested in the responses of general audiences. They have no interest in bridging the possible communication gap between the artist and the public. They would much rather see the continuation of an art that is ghettoized and is the private domain of a select few. The Jewish Museum, by opening up these gateways of communication both through the exhibition and in the range of supporting initiatives, provided a powerful model for a more democratic and responsive art institution."

—Alan Schechner, Mirroring Evil *artist*

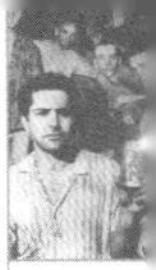

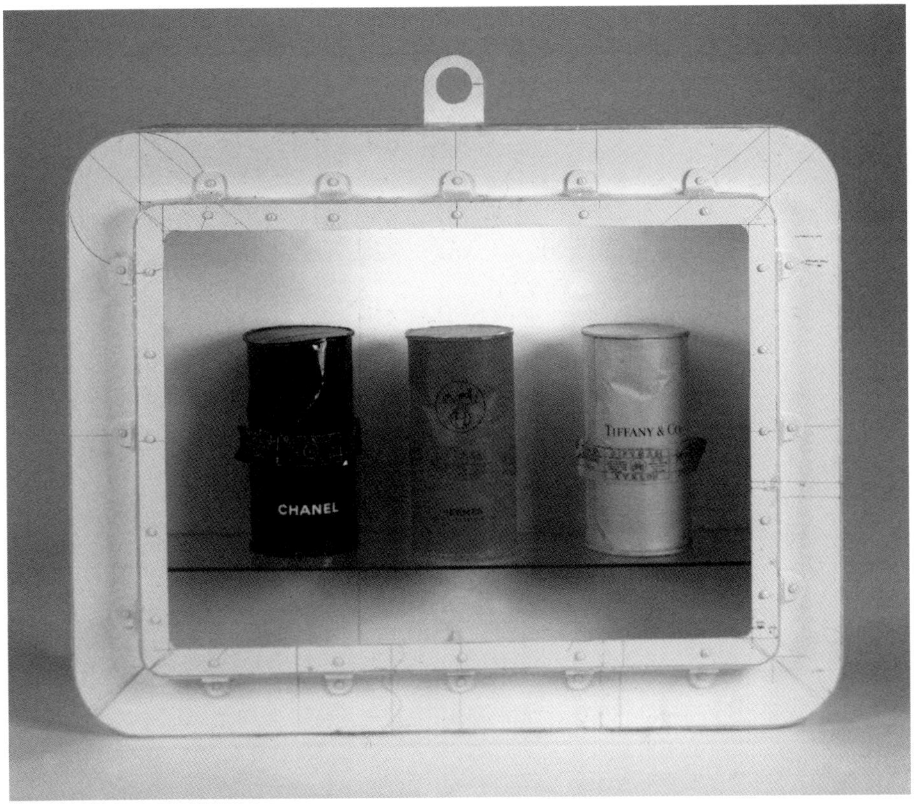

Tom Sachs, Giftgas Giftset. *1998. Courtesy of the artist.*

would actively engage the visitor with individual artworks and the issues the artists had chosen to address. The designers used a variety of strategies, including text panels, subdued warm gray tones for the wall areas, and a small contemplative area that served as the entry to the exhibition. Kershaw's comments in the interim report reveal that the design was intended to offer opportunities for reflection as the visitor moved from piece to piece.

> Initial plans for the exhibition included centrally located "safe rooms," places for visitors to examine the emotions included by the arts, hear or read responses by a variety of commentators, as well as express reactions at computer terminals and response books. After many shifts and adjustments, these rooms were split into a pair of bracketing zones, at the exhibition's entrance and exits.
>
> The design of any museum exhibition is a cooperative process, involving aesthetic, educational, didactic, and security considerations. This particular project anticipated and included far more individual voices and strong opinions. The entire planning and design processes were punctuated by a series of town meeting-type forums, each of which included dissenting as well as encouraging voices from diverse fields. These dialogues aided the process of defining the order and continuity to the exhibit's plan and addressed the fine points of label location and content.

The exhibition was accompanied by a series of carefully crafted text panels that began by restating the core questions raised by the exhibition. Next, an explanatory text panel was designed to accompany each work and included a quote from a scholar, journalist, community member, or survivor. The panel adjacent to Roee Rosen's work is indicative of the high quality of these interpretive materials:

Roee Rosen (Israeli, b. 1963)
***Live and Die as Eva Braun*, 1995**

Mixed media on paper
Courtesy of the Artist, Tel Aviv; Doron Sabag, Tel Aviv; and Eugenio Somaini, Milan.

Through images and texts, Roee Rosen invites us to enter a hallucinatory nightmare, in which we are to imagine ourselves as Adolf Hitler's mistress, Eva Braun. The place is Hitler's Berlin bunker, during the final moments of the Third Reich. The time is immediately after Braun's final sex act with the dictator, when—according to mutual agreement—Hitler will kill her and then commit suicide.

How could Braun have participated in this infernal history? What could her mind have been like? In trying to picture her view of the world, Rosen has created images that initially seem benign. With scalloped edges and simplified forms, they look as if they had come from old photograph albums or children's books—and yet their substance is perverse and morbid.

Through images that are outwardly naïve, sentimental, and charming, we enter a mental space where moral judgment is suspended and brutality becomes seductive. This is how it feels, Rosen suggests, to cavort knowingly with evil.

"Whether imagined in his bunker or out of his bunker, Hitler is today all around us—in our loathing, our fears, our fantasies of power and victimization, our nightmares of vile experience and violent endings. All of which is to say that he has surfaced as a dark presence in the turbulent underside of our dreams and is increasingly to be found in precisely those fictions that are about power, politics, pornography, and mania."

—*Alvin H. Rosenfeld,* Imagining Hitler

"The Jewish Museum, by opening up these gateways of communication both through the exhibition and in the range of supporting initiatives, provided a powerful model for a more democratic and responsive art institution."

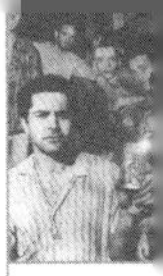

Text panels at the end of the show ask visitors to consider the core questions once more before leaving the museum. These include quotes from scholars and writers, as well as quotes lifted from the media surrounding the project prior to its opening. This captured the public discourse from before the show opened and included differing points of view about the major issues surrounding the exhibition.

The museum staff placed the "talking heads" video in the space at the end of the exhibition. Here the viewer could choose to watch interviews expressing diverse and often opposing points of view of the artists, museum staff, scholars, survivors, and others. Zawatsky writes of this video:

> The video was meant to end the exhibition by adding diverse dialogic viewpoints. It was intended to frame a viewer's discussion on the artists, their intent, and that of community members facing the manifold issues raised by the exhibition as well as the individual works of art. The video was a means to provide visitors with the experience of multiple voices and to help create a setting where they could potentially hear their own voices echoed back.

The museum also produced an exhibition catalogue and brochure to document the project. Catalogue essays were commissioned from leading Holocaust and art history scholars. Along with an introduction by Norman Kleeblatt, each essay offered an in-depth examination of issues pertaining to the artwork and the exhibition. These issues included childhood and evil, representation and the Holocaust, institutional responsibility in exhibiting controversial work, and the ramifications of "trying on" evil. The book also included an in-depth entry on each of the artworks in the exhibition and how each contributes to and advances a multiplicity of possible dialogues. The museum reported an interesting effect of the media's response to the catalogue on exhibition interpretation.

A REFLECTION

"Everyone came to *Mirroring Evil* with a different strong point of view and everyone came. Visitors came because of the publicity; they came because they were curious; they came because they were hostile; they came because they were intrigued...and their questions and comments, in tone and substance, reflected the visitor's viewpoint on entry. No one was unaffected; no one left unchanged. The exhibit, text panels, and docents made the point of the exhibit. The points were understood. The visitors, for the most part, 'got' the exhibition. As a docent, the tensions were perceptibly high. I, too, partook of the publicity, the intrigue, the hostility, and the uncertainty of the public's response. I know *Mirroring Evil* was a success by the attention the visitors paid, and by their questions and thoughtful responses at the end of the tour. *Mirroring Evil* was an educating experience for all participants."

—Linda Sterling, Docent

A REFLECTION

"Every spring, I teach a four-week unit on the Holocaust. The students read the novel *Night* and visit The Jewish Museum and the Museum of Jewish Heritage. This year, I was able to take advantage of the *Mirroring Evil* exhibit as a way of concluding this unit. Even though *Mirroring Evil* is not a Holocaust exhibit *per se*, I felt this was a wonderful way to apply what students had learned to this exhibit.

Before taking the students, I attended an educator's workshop with Peter Nelson and Michelle Asch. It was evident at this workshop that the exhibit created intense dialogue and debate with many of the teachers present. Some educators were very against the idea and would not take their students. I believe that impassioned debate is what all good exhibits should do and I was hoping I could foster this dialogue with my students. Most memorable to me at the workshop was Peter and Michelle's discussion of the Lego boxes. They both made me see the juxtaposition of the innocence of toys with the evil of a concentration camp. I knew that this was one of the pieces that would interest students the most. Many of them still play with toys!

The exhibit did not need a lot of scaffolding with the class that I took. Michelle accompanied us and began with a group discussion of the "Nazi" actors. Students led a discussion on some of the problems that may arise when Hollywood interprets history. I then let them explore on their own for 30 minutes and told them to report back to the group on the piece that really caught their attention. Thirty minutes of free time in a gallery is usually too long for high school students; however, *Mirroring Evil* was engaging them.

Again, the most useful aspect of *Mirroring Evil* was that it provoked insightful debate among my students. One student in particular was not too happy about going. She had read the newspaper articles on the controversy prior to going and had made up her mind. After the trip, she told me she was really glad she came and felt empowered to make her own formed opinions about *Mirroring Evil*."

—David Bally, teacher and participant in the School Program

The media used the book as a weapon with which to ignite a dialogue that became a controversy months before the exhibition opened. Though much of what transpired in those pre-opening months could be understood as a "debate," the media discussed many of the same issues that had been for years at the heart of the exhibition planning stages. For example, by debating whether or not The Jewish Museum should be mounting the exhibition, the topics of "Who can speak for the Holocaust?" and "What are the limits of representation?" were of prime significance. Quoting the media on text panels throughout the exhibition incorporated many of their ideas and comments, and this was also shared with the general public during the pre-opening months."

The exhibition brochure was meant to inform the public that the project, with a varied menu of educational and public components, was conceived as more than an exhibition. It featured the entire scope of the project by listing and explaining each of its components, each of the institutional partners, and a roster of dialogue opportunities through a calendar of public programs.

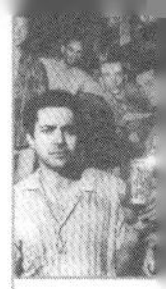

The Warning Text

As already noted, the exhibition generated significant controversy before it ever opened. Holocaust survivors demanded that four of the works be removed from the exhibition, a demand that the museum rejected. During the negotiations, CLAL played a significant role in crafting a compromise that would address the concerns of the survivors and their families while protecting the integrity of the museum. Ultimately, the decision was made to post the following warning that included directions on how to leave the exhibition prior to entering the section where some of the work that was identified as most disturbing was located.

> Some Holocaust survivors have been disturbed by the works of art shown beyond this point. Visitors may choose to avoid these works by exiting the door to the left.[8]

[8] The three pieces located on the other side were Libera's "LEGO Concentration Camp," Sach's "Giftgas Giftset," and Schechner's "Self Portrait at Buchenwald."

This decision was applauded by some in the mainstream media and the Jewish press as evidence of the museum's interest in ameliorating the genuine pain that some survivors felt at being asked to view the works. At the same time, this text and the interpretation offered through videos, wall texts, and labels, taken in concert with the opportunity to avoid certain works of art, could be seen as attempts to intervene in the viewer's experiential engagement with the artworks. The issue of the role of interpretation in preparing the audience, defusing negative responses, or explaining artistic, curatorial, or institutional intentionality is an ongoing discussion in the cultural community. The experiences from this exhibition offer opportunities for new research on this controversial, multifaceted discourse.

Dialogic Intent and Design

From December 2001–March 2002, The Jewish Museum organized a number of staff training and dialogue opportunities. The museum describes the structure and function of these trainings:

> This [staff training and dialogue opportunities] gave the entire institution an opportunity to learn and engage in the exhibition and project as a whole, to discuss the issues, to pose questions, to familiarize themselves with [the] art, and to voice their concerns... Subsequent training sessions focused on empathy and dialogic opportunities in which several methods were discussed regarding how to manage general visitors as well as long-standing museum members who might voice their disapproval of the exhibition or the museum.

These sessions were instrumental in helping to frame the issues that were seen as relevant and important to the museum and its staff. The staff report that these discussions allowed them to voice their concerns regarding vandalism and safety and were seen to have been critical to the project. The project interim report, which was submitted weeks into the exhibition's controversy, provided an important insight that arose from the staff meetings.

> At times the general mood became one of helplessness that resulted from the museum not having any prior antecedents in the area of public controversy and from not having anticipated the quantity and quality of responses the museum and staff would have to process.

As part of its dialogue program, the museum developed an education guide that served as a curriculum resource for educators who were interested in bringing their students to the exhibition as a way to integrate the artwork into the class curriculum. Michelle Asche, manager for school programs and outreach, describes the functionality of the education guide:

> The guide was designed to assist teachers in their intentions towards incorporating themes from the artwork into their class curriculum...with historical background, related quotes, questions, follow-up activities, a glossary of terms, and a selection of readings.

Three educator seminars were designed to offer teachers the opportunity to see the exhibition and address its themes through dialogue with their colleagues prior to bringing their students. Teachers were required to attend a seminar prior to bringing their students to the exhibition. The workshops were planned with Peter Nelson from Facing History and Ourselves. The museum also put a system in place that allowed it to respond to every letter or telephone call through one of several form letters that were developed in response to visitor concerns. In addition, 15 student groups (294 participants in total) and 84 adult groups (1,029 participants in total) requested private tours of the exhibition and discussion with the education or curatorial staff.

PUBLIC DIALOGUE

The original plan called for a series of public panels and forums that included speakers and respondents followed by questions and answers from the audience. Examples of these programs included:

March 14, 2002—*Encountering Evil: An Artists' Roundtable* featured four artists—Kuball, Libera, Borland, and Rosen—and was moderated by Karen Michel. There was some concern that the questions from the audience would be difficult to handle, and the museum decided to ask the audience to write the questions on index cards that were then handed to the moderator. This allowed the moderator to have some control over the tone and content of the questions that she focused on, the "trajectory and context for the work on display vis-à-vis an entire career."

March 21—*The Root of All Evil* panel participants changed, as two of the three original speakers cancelled for health-related reasons (Robert J. Lifton and Marguerite Feitlowitz). Shortly before the exhibition began, Rob Rosenbaum withdrew in objection to the content. The panel was reconstituted to present Melvin Bukiet, author of *While the Messiah Tarries;* Burton L. Visotsky, of the Jewish Theological Seminary of America; and James E. Young, of the University of Massachusetts at Amherst. The final report, dated September 18, 2002, includes a statement by Aviva Weintraub, director of media and public programs:

> Ordinarily in such a case, the museum would have cancelled the program, contacted people who had ordered tickets, and issued refunds. However, under the circumstances, I felt strongly that canceling a program would be misinterpreted in the press... We did offer refunds to anyone who was disappointed at not seeing the original speakers; approximately three people asked for a refund.

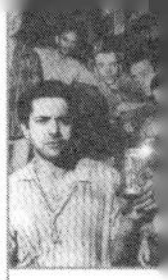

Karen Michel also moderated the second panel and writes in the final report:

> Discussion was lively, noncombative, and generally led participants and audience to a sense of understanding, not blame.

April 11—*Transgressive Commodities: A Symposium in Response to the Exhibition Mirroring Evil: Nazi Imagery/Recent Art* originally comprised James Young, professor of English and chair of Judaic studies, University of Massachusetts, Amherst; Lisa Saltzman, associate professor of history of art, Bryn Mawr College; Alan Schechner, one of the artists from the exhibit; and Emory University professor and renowned Holocaust scholar Deborah Lipstadt, Dorot Professor of Modern Jewish History and Holocaust Studies and director of Jewish studies. Dr. Lipstadt withdrew her support for the show and chose not to attend.

"By returning to the shared experience of the exhibit, and encouraging visitors to ground their remarks in the particulars of that experience, I was usually able to contain and redirect more general provocations into constructive channels—into genuine dialogue."

April 25—*The Banalities of Evil,* a panel held at The New School, focused on Hannah Arendt's *Eichmann in Jerusalem*, as well as her *Origins of Totalitarianism*, to provide the background for our re-examination of some of her controversial speculations on the nature of radical evil and "the banality of evil."

May 28—*Moral Ambiguity in the Representation of Evil* was the first of three public forums in which the format was designed to allow speakers and audience to engage in a more interactive conversation. Lindenbaum reports that this was the most successful of the three forums, although only 40 people attended. Ellen Handler Spitz, who contributed an essay for the exhibition catalogue, participated in this forum and writes:

> As is often the case in such gatherings, there were one or two highly vociferous attendees who seemed to need to dominate. However, we managed to find ways to curtail their "long-windedness" sufficiently, I think, to provide time for others to express themselves. One aspect of the discussion that intrigued me was that the exhibit came to be used by many as a jumping-off place for a discussion on related [issues,] (i.e., children's education and contemporary politics and definitions of good and evil). Few people seemed to want to discuss the works of art themselves.

June 13—Screening of *The Night Porter* at The New School drew a large and diverse audience. A pre-film talk by Susannah Heschel outlined a variety of issues raised by the film. After the screening, the dialogue addressed issues of how many Nazis, particularly former SS officers, were able to lead normal middle class lives in post-war Vienna.

In March 2002, the museum added an additional component in the form of daily public dialogues. Mohini Shapero was hired as the facilitator for the daily dialogues and for the more occasional dialogues for targeted constituent groups. The decision to add a daily dialogue component and to hire Shapero came late in the planning for the exhibition. That March, Ruth Beesch wrote to [Animating Democracy], requesting additional financial support to expand the dialogue component of the project. Beesch positioned her request in the context of the heated controversy that had arisen prior to the exhibition's opening.

[9] Letter dated March 4, 2002, from Ruth Beesch, The Jewish Museum, to Barbara Schaffer Bacon, co-director, Animating Democracy.

> As you know, we have been attempting to engage a number of those opposed to *Mirroring Evil*...by inviting them into the museum for a dialogue. Unfortunately, it has been a deaf dialogue thus far, but it has made us realize that we need a safe place within the museum (and outside of the exhibition galleries) to encourage dialogue on a daily basis for visitors to the exhibition.[9]

A total of 67 one-hour dialogues were offered, in which approximately 475 visitors participated. Groups ranged in size from one to 30 participants. While the facilitator did not gather demographic data, anecdotal reports suggest that the participants spanned a wide spectrum of age, ethnicity, and background. Survivors were described as among the most eloquent participants, and their feelings about the exhibition ranged from anger to appreciation. Shapero described her strategy to structure the daily dialogue activity.

> My strategy was always to begin by centering the discussion on the art and then proceeding to more general associations and concerns, often refocusing attention on particular works as a way of grounding a conversation that threatened to devolve into grandstanding. This was a constant challenge... The exhibit, after all, was the common experience that brought all of us together; it formed a communal link between diverse participants in the group. By returning to the shared experience of the exhibit, and encouraging visitors to ground their remarks in the particulars of that experience, I was usually able to contain and redirect more general provocations into constructive channels—into genuine dialogue.

Interestingly, she also notes that she began her experience as facilitator convinced that she should employ a formal structure for managing the dialogue activities. She developed dialogue guidelines, including an index card activity that asked each visitor to write down the piece that had the greatest impact. After collecting the cards, she read them aloud as a stimulus to the dialogue activity. Ultimately, she learned that this rigid format, while effective in some situations, was not always appropriate.

THE NATIONAL JEWISH CENTER FOR LEARNING AND LEADERSHIP'S REFLECTIONS ON ITS PARTNERSHIP WITH THE JEWISH MUSEUM

As CLAL's Vice President Rabbi Brad Hirschfield observed in an op-ed for *The Jewish Week*, the exhibition raised profoundly important ethical questions that hit vital nerves in Jewish communities and that highlighted deep generational and ideological divides. CLAL has always provided forums for discussions that respect and confront these divides. The work we did with The Jewish Museum/Animating Democracy Initiative on *Mirroring Evil* challenged us to structure such forums in new ways—through engaging particular pieces of art, as well as the controversy around them; and through playing the role of mediator between, on the one hand, the exhibition and the museum, and, on the other, various segments of the Jewish community.

Exploring how best to spark conversation around visual art was an apt project for us, given

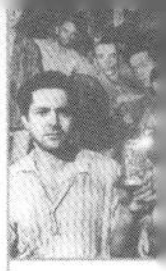

that we are always looking for new methodologies—from using traditional Jewish texts in new ways to future-oriented debates that take their cue from modes of thinking pioneered in the business world—to open up people's thinking and to stimulate real exchange of ideas about critical ethical questions. In fact, we have been giving a good deal of thought, in other contexts, to the potential of art—including music, film, and theater—to help us build meaningful programming.

We knew from the beginning that the questions the art in *Mirroring Evil* posed about "ownership" over the Holocaust; the power of media to narrate, distort, and persuade; and the processes of identification with perpetrators or victims could make for explosive reactions. The question, with each constituency, was how best to balance "framing" the conversation (including introductions by CLAL faculty as well as commentary by panelists and curators) so that it would remain focused while, at the same time, leaving room for open, participatory conversation. Indeed, we felt that conversations in which participants were urged to focus more closely on the particularities of the art would ultimately be more open than purely free ranging discussions, which could end up merely rehashing familiar controversies about "Holocaust representation" or "Holocaust memory" in familiar, general terms.

By the time the exhibition opened, this balancing act between framing and openness had been further complicated by the controversy that played out in the press, which sparked interest in the exhibition but, in a sense, threatened to overshadow the art itself and to pre-set the terms of the discussions. For each program, we tried to build in time for setting out some central questions (not necessarily those deemed most interesting in the press coverage), contemplating the art, pooling participants' reactions, and facilitating discussion and debate in small groups. In each, we experimented with the order and balance of these components.

With regard to the framing/openness issue, the public program, which was the most ambitious and multifaceted of the three programs, seemed to work particularly well. In part, this was, we think, as Norman Kleeblatt observed in his remarks that evening, because the event actually brought the art outside the space of the museum into a more neutral setting (this was possible, too, because of the mobile nature of the two pieces). Perhaps it was also because the conversation was focused around particular pieces of art, and particular themes; perhaps it was because we designed the event so that groups of participants had time to share their own reactions with each other before hearing from the panel of speakers. The speakers' ideas, in turn, then served as additional fodder for the second segment of the groups' conversations.

The public program, as the most complicated of the events and the one that enlisted the involvement of the most outside people, was productive for us in another unexpected way. It was something of an experiment for us, as most of our programs tend to be geared toward particular constituencies. We were quite pleased with it, however, and would like to undertake more such programs in the future.

Before the program, we held a meeting for curators, speakers, and facilitators—some of whom had worked with us in other contexts, some of whom were joining us for the first time—to meet each other, view the art, and discuss the goals and methods of the program. The meeting turned out to be one of the most interesting conversations we convened in the course of the grant. It was a diverse and lively group of people, and both the conversation about the two works of art and the conversation about the program's design were thought- provoking and productive. We had already done a good deal of careful planning and deliberately left room for input from speakers and facilitators as well. Though this more democratic approach demanded more time from those who participated, taking everyone's experience and ideas into consideration made, ultimately, for a stronger program.

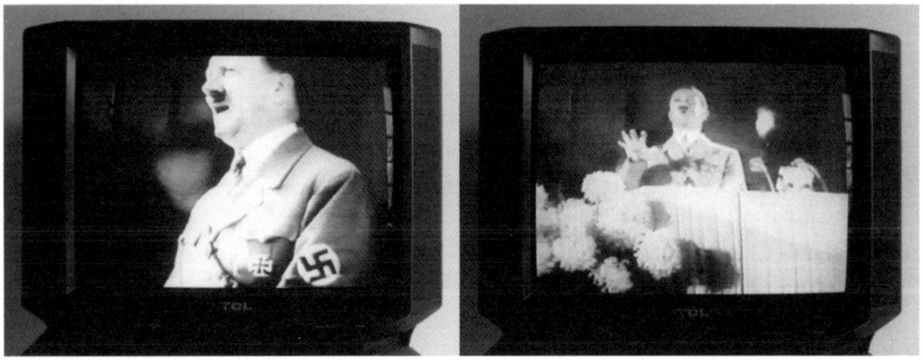

Boaz Arad, Hebrew Lesson. *2000. Courtesy of the artist.*

> Through experience, I discovered that it was important to adapt this structure... Indeed responding to the particular audience with flexibility and sensitivity was the most crucial element to running a successful dialogue...

In assessing the success of this component of the dialogue program, it is important to note that the issue of daily dialogues had, in fact, been explored several months prior to the request to Animating Democracy for additional funding, but for logistical and space reasons, it had not proven feasible.[10] While it is certainly true that this element of the dialogue project was instituted as a reaction to pressure from media controversy and the concerns of Holocaust survivors, it was nevertheless an important step forward in the museum's attempts to craft a truly open environment where visitors could express their responses to the exhibition and its content. Information gathered from the final report and through discussion with the museum staff indicates that it was successful in addressing some of the concerns around offering space for visitors to discuss their feelings with others. Of course, the flaw in this approach lies in generalizing anything from the responses of this self-selected population. However, taken as one stream of dialogic activity among many, it appears to have met its objectives.

[10] In fact, in January 2002, this strategy had also been discussed with The Jewish Museum by their colleagues at The Andy Warhol Museum, another Animating Democracy Lab participant that had used the strategy of daily dialogues and "safe spaces" with great success in its project, *Without Sanctuary.*

As a partner in *Mirroring Evil,* The National Jewish Center for Learning and Leadership (CLAL) organized three dialogue programs. The first, on March 20, 2002, was a program for approximately 40 Jewish community leaders and philanthropists. The evening combined a private viewing of the art together with museum curators and a chance for participants to reflect, in small groups facilitated by CLAL faculty, on the issues the art raised for them, as well as for the institutions and communities in which they are involved. The second, held on June 3, 2002, was a public event at The Vera List Center for Art and Politics at The New School. Called *Is Nothing Sacred in a Consumer Culture? Images of the Holocaust in the Age of Advertising,* this program was designed to spark conversation around two of the exhibition's particularly provocative pieces, Alan Schechner's "It's the Real Thing: Self-Portrait at Buchenwald" and Maciej Toporowicz's "Obsession." The third program was held on June 11, 2002. For this event, CLAL brought rabbis and religious leaders from other faiths—as part of CLAL's Religious Leaders Symposium—to the museum for a viewing followed by facilitated dialogue, focusing on the issues the art raises for religious communities and institutions.

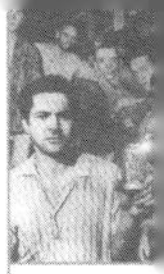

These efforts challenged CLAL to structure such forums in new ways—through engaging particular pieces of art, as well as the controversy around them—and through playing the role of mediator between, on the one hand, the exhibition and the museum and, on the other, various segments of the Jewish community. (See the sidebar for CLAL's thoughtful analysis of these arts-based dialogues.)

THE CONTROVERSY

Conversations with The Jewish Museum staff during and after *Mirroring Evil* reveal an organizational culture that has encouraged the staff to engage in open, sincere, and introspective examination of every phase of the exhibition from the initial decision to explore this highly sensitive subject matter to the responses and controversy that erupted months before the exhibition ever opened. Norman Kleeblatt reports that the museum's decision to schedule *Mirroring Evil* to run for three months rather than the normal four was made in recognition that the difficult subject matter might be problematic for some of its constituents.[11] There is also no doubt that the media played a role as a stimulus to controversy and as a tool for those who were interested in disrupting the exhibition for their own purposes.

[11] Norman Kleeblatt and Joanna Lindenbaum, conversation with curators, The Jewish Museum, January 12, 2002.

An in-depth analysis of the media reception regarding the exhibition is beyond the scope of this case study. However, the media did play a role in stimulating public discussion (perhaps a more descriptive term than dialogue in this case) regarding the exhibition. There is always the hope that the media will serve as the portal to the marketplace of ideas where free exchange of diverse points of view can lead to knowledge and understanding. Sadly, there were only rare occurrences where the discourse around the exhibition added much to the public's understanding of the intentionality of either the artists or the museum. Rather, it soon became clear that much of the New York media served as the purveyor of a generally unproductive discourse and did not address the complex social, cultural, and aesthetic issues raised by the exhibition.

All of this evokes the memories of the turbulent 1990s, a period that has come to be known as the "culture wars." It was a decade when contemporary art was at the center of a well-orchestrated campaign by the Religious Right designed to erode support for public funding for the arts. In this case, the media controversy began with one incendiary spark from an unlikely source, a *Wall Street Journal* reporter who appeared to purposefully generate a climate of misunderstanding and controversy that raged in the three months before the exhibition ever opened. It was a battle over art that no one had yet seen. It was a controversy about the idea of an exhibition and as such it allowed all sides to construct their bunkers and take their positions notwithstanding any real reception or analysis of the artworks involved. It was, therefore, the quintessential art world controversy.

...the media controversy began with one incendiary spark from an unlikely source, a **Wall Street Journal** *reporter who appeared to purposefully generate a climate of misunderstanding and controversy that raged in the three months before the exhibition ever opened.*

Joan Rosenbaum, Helen Goldsmith Menschel director of The Jewish Museum, released a statement just prior to the opening of the exhibition in March 2002:

> We recognize that there are people, some of them Holocaust survivors, who may not wish to view this exhibition, or who, in viewing it, may be angry or distressed. However, as an art museum that presents all of Jewish culture, we

reaffirm our commitment to showing works of contemporary artists who have used images of the Nazi era to make a powerful and timely investigation of the nature of evil.[12]

[12] Quoted in Michael Elkin, "Constructing a Controversy," *Jewish Exponent* (PA), April 11, 2002.

What could have precipitated such an extraordinary statement by the leader of a cultural institution? In some sense, the statement reflected the fact that The Jewish Museum's exhibition did not appear in a vacuum.

In October 1999, *Sensation: Young British Artists from the Saatchi Collection*, an exhibition that included 90 paintings, sculpture, photographs, and installations by 42 artists, opened at the Brooklyn Museum. One week before the scheduled opening, Republican Mayor Rudolph Giuliani told the Brooklyn Museum to cancel the exhibition or lose its annual $7 million City Hall grant. Giuliani was particularly offended by the work of Chris Ofili, "Virgin Mary, Elephant Dung." The mayor had not seen the exhibition himself, but made his decision based upon an examination of the show's catalogue.

It may have been inevitable then that when the media learned that The Jewish Museum was planning to organize an exhibition of work that utilized Nazi imagery, comparisons to *Sensation* would begin to surface. Michael Kimmelman of the *New York Times* writes in his preview article:

> Detractors see it as just another *Sensation*, but pushing the buttons of Jews this time instead of Roman Catholics... This time it's Jews who are asking why The Jewish Museum, of all places, should present art that offends Jews.[13]

[13] Michael Kimmelman, "Critic's Notebook: Jewish Museum Show Looks Nazis in the Face and Creates a Fuss," *New York Times*, January 29, 2002.

The pre-opening discourse that swirled around *Mirroring Evil* was precipitated by a reading from the exhibition catalogue at the museum in late November, where several Holocaust survivors became agitated at the proposed content. Lisa Gubernick of the *Wall Street Journal* learned about the survivors' response, and her January 10, 2002, article began with the opening salvo of what was to become a theme of the media coverage:

> An art exhibition headed for New York could become the next art-world *Sensation*. That 1999 exhibition at the Brooklyn Museum of Art featured a painting of the Virgin Mary splattered with dung, drawing fire from Catholics, including former mayor Rudolph Giuliani, among others. This show's exhibits include LEGO concentration camp kits, swastika-bedecked kitten figures, and sculptures of notorious Auschwitz doctor Josef Mengele—and is all the more controversial given its setting: the Jewish Museum.[14]

[14] Lisa Gubernick, "Coming Museum Show with Nazi Theme Stirs New York's Artworld," *Wall Street Journal*, January 10, 2002.

Other New York media outlets picked up the story. The *New York Times* art critic Michael Kimmelman in January 2002 stated:

> It has not been lost on officials at The Jewish Museum that sight unseen the show has probably infuriated some of the people who have helped make *The Producers* Broadway's hottest ticket... All is not fair in the culture wars. Such is the burden on a museum tackling touchy work.[15]

[15] Michael Kimmelman, "Critic's Notebook: Jewish Museum Show Looks Nazis in the Face and Creates a Fuss," *New York Times*, January 29, 2002.

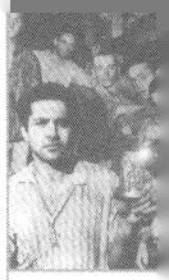

Sarah Boxer's interview with Kleeblatt in the *New York Times* on February 6, 2002, offered the curator the opportunity to set forth his aesthetic and conceptual point of view. Much of the article restates the intentionality described in Kleeblatt's essay, but at the close of the piece, the writer raises a series of highly provocative questions in response to Kleeblatt's assertions that the participating artists are vigilant in their exploration of how Nazi imagery has been appropriated by popular culture. The writer posed the questions:

> The artists may be vigilant about the images that have shaped them but how vigilant can they be about the effects of their own imagery? And how vigilant can a curator really be? Indeed, how can anyone tell the difference between the work of a real Nazi sympathizer and a hip contemporary artist playing with the fire of popular culture?[16]

[16] Sarah Boxer, "Man Behind a Museum Tempest: A Curator's Defense of Nazi Imagery," *New York Times*, February 6, 2002.

Kleeblatt responded:

> "I wouldn't show any neo-Nazi works," Mr. Kleeblatt said, recoiling as if singed by a flame. "I am responsible."[17]

[17] Ibid.

New York newspapers offered space to a variety of individuals to express their strongly held views. In the February 4, 2002, edition of the *New York Post*, Menachem Z. Rosensaft, founding chairman of the International Network of Jewish Holocaust Survivors, wrote an op-ed under the title "The 'Art' of Desecration." The piece began with language that was inflammatory even for the notorious rhetorical excess that characterizes the *Post*:

> At first glance, it seems nothing more than yet another example of tastelessness masquerading as culture—the crass, in-your-face, vulgarity that now routinely replaces talent as an effective means of attracting readers, viewers, and audiences... I am not shocked that there are artists who ridicule the Holocaust and demean the experiences of its victims. Nor would I have been particularly surprised if an exhibition like *Mirroring Evil* had been sponsored by the Holocaust-denying Institute for Historical Review or some other anti-Semitic outfit. The outrage is that a respected mainstream Jewish cultural institution is legitimizing the banalization of the Holocaust.[18]

[18] Menachem Rosensaft, "The 'Art' of Desecration," *New York Post*, February 4, 2002.

And so the stage was set for what will be the most commonly heard complaint from Holocaust survivors and those who represent them: how could The Jewish Museum do this to us?

And so the stage was set for what will be the most commonly heard complaint from Holocaust survivors and those who represent them: how could The Jewish Museum do this to us? Their contention arose from an expectation that they have come to expect that they may be assaulted from without, but to have that which they hold most dear assailed by their own is the gravest form of insult and injury.

The January 18, 2002, "Forward Forum," a feature of the Jewish newspaper, *Forward*, presented two texts under the title of "Demystifying Nazism, or Trivializing its Victims? A Debate." The first text, "How Pseudo-Artists Desecrate the Holocaust," again gave voice to Menachem Rosensaft. The second, by catalogue contributor Professor James E. Young, was titled. "Museum Show Truthfully Probes Society's Fascination with Evil and the Second World War." Both individuals would become familiar spokespersons for the opposing points of view of the exhibition, Rosensaft in his call for a boycott and Young as one of the defenders of the conceptual framework chosen by the museum in which to situate the work.

Rosensaft closes his statement with a message:

> The Jewish Museum now has a choice to make. It can admit that it has made a mistake and withdraw this ill-conceived exhibition, or it can reap the dire consequences of going ahead with it. If *Mirroring Evil* opens March 17 as scheduled, Holocaust survivors and their families, as well as others with similar moral sensitivities will not remain silent. Loud demonstrations and pickets may be the least of the museum's problems.[19]

[19] *Forward*, January 18, 2002.

He goes on to say that the problems he foresees will be the damage to the museum's reputation, but for many who read the missive, the threat was far more serious. The claim that demonstrations and pickets may be the least of the museum's problems was read by many as a serious threat, and the museum took extraordinary security measures throughout the exhibition.

James Young's piece begins with a restatement of the curatorial intent of the exhibition:

> Until recently, most "Holocaust art" has concentrated, understandably, on the victims of Nazi crimes—as a way to commemorate them, name them, extol them, bring them back from the dead... For a new generation of artists, some of them Jewish and Israeli, the only thing more shocking than the images of suffering victims is the depravity of the human beings who caused such suffering... These artists challenge us to confront the faces of evil, which, if truth be told, look rather more like us than the victims the Nazis left behind.[20]

[20] James Young, "Museum Show Truthfully Probes Society's Fascination with Evil," *Forward*, January 18, 2002.

Young reminds the readers of their responsibility to face the critical questions raised by these artists regarding the role of evil in society and also regarding the role of a cultural institution to exhibit these works in a respectful context that avoids sensationalizing the very evil it seeks to expose. To do so, however, requires participation.

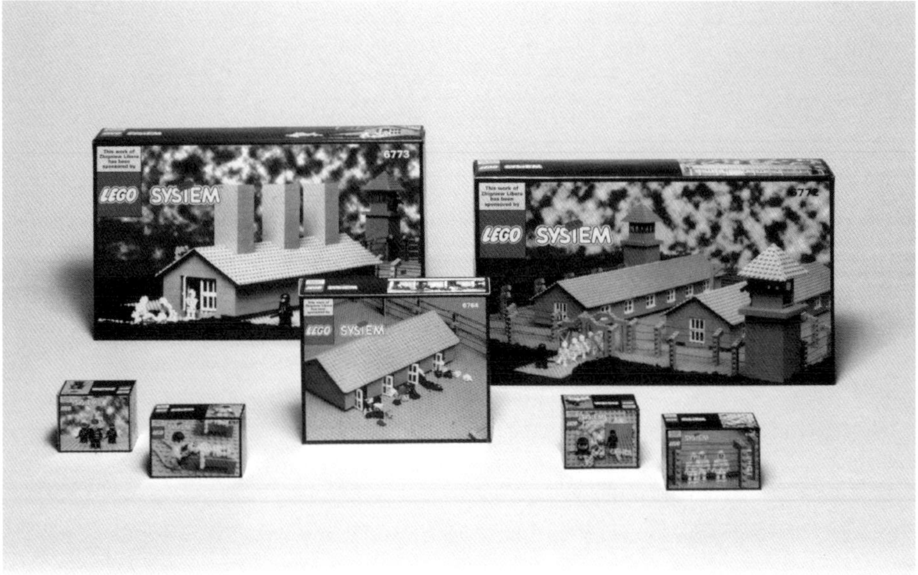

Zbigniew Libera, LEGO Concentration Camp Set (detail). *1996. Courtesy of the artist.*

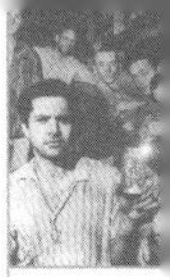

A REFLECTION

"The Museum's public relations campaign was an effort to gain the support, or at least the tolerance, of those people who did not instantly make up their minds about *Mirroring Evil*. The Jewish Museum's staff and its public relations consultant, The Kreisberg Group, made every effort to moderate the tone of these broadcasts and articles, to protect the Museum's image, and to supply journalists with material that would make the Museum's messages about *Mirroring Evil* a part of the news stories. The Museum's messages were consistently and widely disseminated; open-minded audiences were provided with the contextual information they needed to judge *Mirroring Evil* for themselves; the Museum ensured that objections to the exhibition were answered appropriately in public outlets; the curatorial integrity of the Museum and the value of its commitment to contemporary art were upheld. To an extent, these efforts were successful—however, the controversy on the whole proved to be uncontrollable. It influenced for the worse much (not all) of the other exhibition coverage."

—Anne Scher, director of communications, The Jewish Museum

> In the end, viewers of the exhibition and readers of its catalogue will have to decide for themselves—but only after they have actually seen the exhibition.[21]

[21] Ibid.

It is clear that this "debate" added little to the opportunities for dialogue. The reader does not know whether Young and Rosensaft had the opportunity to read each other's pieces prior to publication, thereby offering a "call and response" format for the debate. The texts do seem to reflect that each had a script to follow—Rosensaft, emotional and righteous; Young, cool and academic—and this format would continue in the parallel streams of discourse that were to follow in the weeks and months ahead.

It was not only the Jewish press that wondered about the role the media played in precipitating and manipulating the controversy. From Los Angeles, the *Los Angles Times* art critic, Christopher Knight, had his own theory about how the media functions in its relationship to the art world:

> It was, in fact, a business bible that kicked off the ruckus over The Jewish Museum show. The *Wall Street Journal* ran a story on the front page of its second section on January 10, nine full weeks before the exhibition opened. It began, "An art exhibition headed for New York could become the next art-world *Sensation*..." As a rule of thumb, news stories report what *did* happen not what *could* happen. A sensation story saying that *Mirroring Evil* could become a media scandal is what is known as a self-fulfilling prophesy.[22]

[22] Christopher Knight, "The Evil that Museums Do," *Los Angeles Times*, April 7, 2002.

The controversy spilled over into the media outside of New York City as exemplified by a piece in the February 24, 2002, issue of *The Washington Post* by Alan Cooperman, "Art or Insult: A Dialogue Shaped by the Holocaust." Cooperman outlines the critical questions raised not by the artwork but by the protests that took place before the show even opened.

> Are there places where art simply should not go, events that are too raw to be depicted in a painting, too far-reaching to be reduced to the confines of a photographic frame? Beside the issue of each work's technical merit, whose standards of acceptability should apply and what is the curators' responsibility? Looking ahead, how will we react when the events of Sept. 11 are held up for reflection in the watercolors, novels, or video clips of future generations?[23]

[23] Alan Cooperman, "Art or Insult, A Dialogue Shaped by the Holocaust," *Washington Post*, February 24, 2002.

Other reviewers expressed a far more sympathetic view of the exhibition. Simon Houpt, writing in the *Globe and Mail* from Toronto, Canada, on March 20, 2002, begins his review by comparing *Mirroring Evil* not to *Sensation* but to *The Producers*.

> Some cultural coincidences are too piquant for words. Sunday afternoon, New York's Upper East Side neighborhood rage with the shouts of angry protestors trying to shame visitors going to the opening of the hotly contested exhibition *Mirroring Evil* at The Jewish Museum. Meanwhile only a couple of kilometers away, Matthew Broderick and Nathan Lane sailed through the final performance of their year-long run in Mel Brooks's *The Producers,* a Broadway musical that takes enormous pleasure in those hilarious clowns of the 20th century, the Nazis. Cheers and a standing ovation greeted their final bows.[24]

[24] Simon Houpt, review, *Globe and Mail, Toronto*, March 20, 2002.

CONCLUSIONS

When an art museum ventures into taboo subject matter as part of its intent to facilitate a deeper understanding of complex issues, the waters can become treacherous. From the outset, there was an understanding that the work chosen for *Mirroring Evil* was challenging not only in its choice of subject matter but also in the cool, highly intellectualized manner in which it approached its emotionally charged content. The Jewish Museum staff and trustees were acutely aware that their normal public programming would not suffice, and they were eager to explore new strategies to encourage civic dialogue that would begin with the artworks and evolve toward an exploration of the consequences of society's complicity in the face of the unspeakable. The museum offered its audiences the opportunity to experience art being created by a new generation of artists, who sought to break through old boundaries to address this difficult, yet timely, subject. The rewards of programming of this kind lie in the possibility that while audiences may well be initially offended; at the same time, they may also be receptive to new ways of thinking. Museum leadership crafted critical questions that framed the interpretive materials, public programs, and civic dialogue activities. The dialogic approach was also evident in the museum's commitment to find new ways of working within its own walls, including establishing communication between and among departments and across traditional institutional hierarchies. Unfortunately, the museum's efforts to create free and open exchange of ideas were somewhat hampered by an over-zealous media and a variety of players, many of whom were eager to have their 15 minutes in the spotlight. As is often the case, many who expressed the most strident criticism announced with equal fervor that they had made their judgment without ever seeing the exhibition.

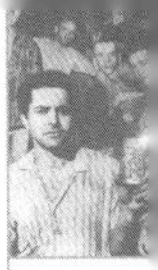

It is tempting to question whether the compromises made by The Jewish Museum in responding to the concerns expressed by Holocaust survivors were congruent with its mission to explore Jewish culture and engage in cultural outreach. In the post culture wars environment, we drift easily into our respective scripts, casting all the players in an art controversy as villains or heroes depending upon one's political point of view. The lessons from *Mirroring Evil* reveal that whether one's worldview demands that "artists must *always* be completely free to express their views," or that "arts organizations must *never* transgress into forbidden territory," reality rarely resides comfortably within the boundaries of "always/never" land. Norman Kleeblatt acknowledges the museum's initial instinct to defend and protect itself from the turgid rhetoric of media pundits, politicians, and demagogues—all of whom were willing to exploit Holocaust survivors for their own purposes. The instinct was to close ranks, build a bunker around the building, and focus efforts on damage control. Kleeblatt believes that the decision to enlist CLAL to facilitate a face-to-face dialogue with those opposed to the exhibition helped the staff come to understand that, for the survivors and their families, the representation of the perpetrators of evil within the walls of The Jewish Museum was both a betrayal of trust and an effort to diminish the enormity of their suffering.[25] It is from this perspective, rather than from one of capitulation and expediency, that the impulse toward compromise was born.

[25] Norman Kleeblatt and Joanna Lindenbaum, conversation with curators, The Jewish Museum, January 12, 2004.

It is important to acknowledge *Mirroring Evil* is only the first step in the Jewish community's efforts to examine the nature of the evil and the responses to it that have so formed its character since the Holocaust. An examination of the social, political, and art historical scholarship that is now beginning to emerge as part of the critical response to the exhibition will reveal whether the discourse will continue. Nevertheless, The Jewish Museum clearly believes that it weathered the storm. Perhaps this is best captured in the remarks of Director Joan Rosenbaum, when she writes:

> [We now have] the knowledge that the public is willing, if they will come to the exhibit, to engage in a dialogue with the works, with each other, docents, scholars and educators. We found an eagerness to read, understand, and form opinions and communicate them among those people, who in spite of the press, were willing to come to the door. This is stimulating knowledge and gives us inspiration for other exhibitions that will keep this dialogue going. The museum was "opened up" in an unusual way.

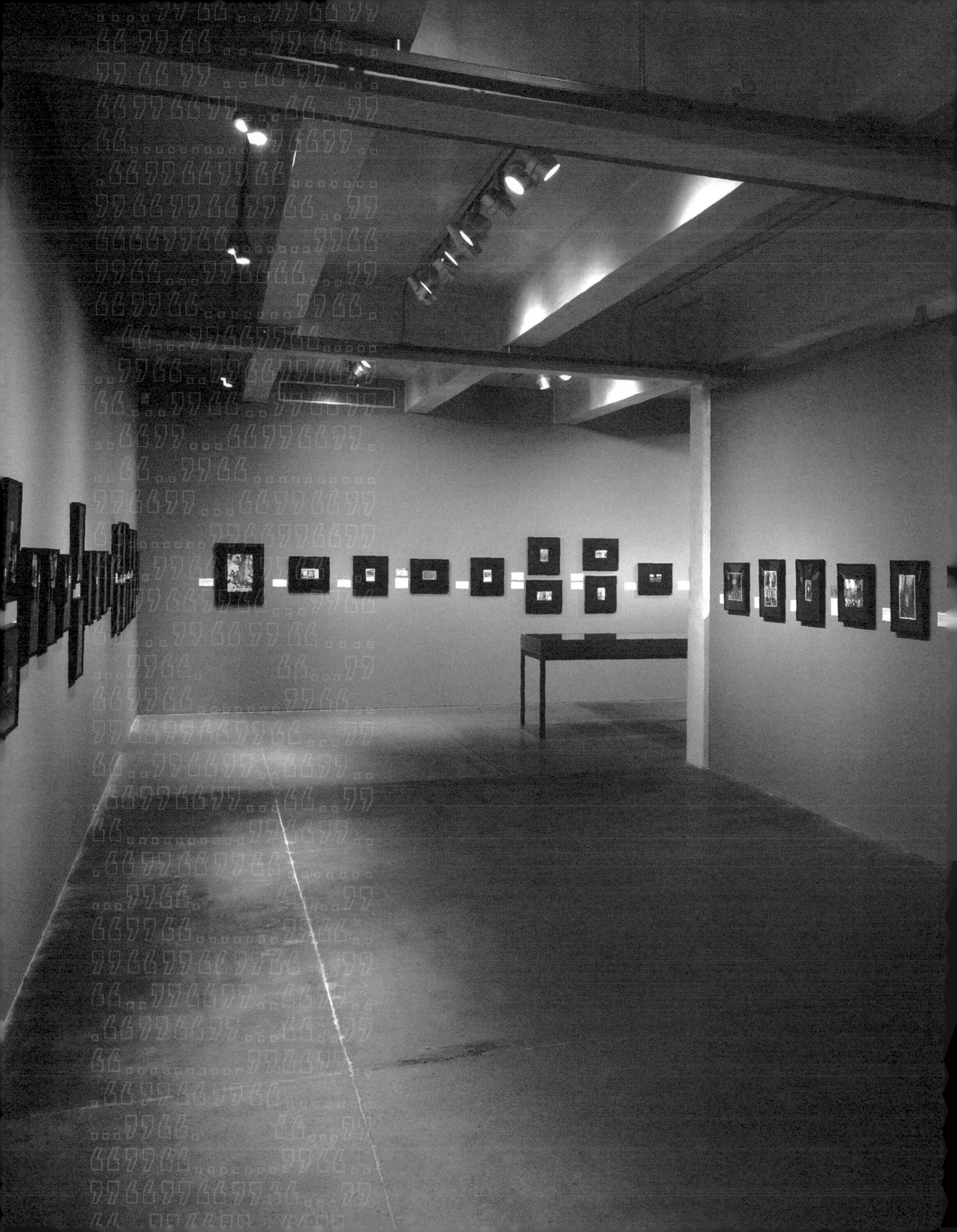

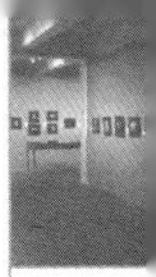

3 The Andy Warhol Museum

⁝⁝⁝ MUSEUM AS ARTIST: CREATIVE, DIALOGIC, & CIVIC PRACTICE

JESSICA GOGAN

As I see it, a museum is an answer to a fundamental question: what does it mean to be a human being?... The most vital function of museums is to balance, to regulate what we might call the symbolic ecology of cultures, by putting forward alternative views and thus keeping choice and critical dialogue alive.[1]

—Neil Postman

In his famous 1822 painting, *The Artist in His Museum,* Charles Wilson Peale, full of Enlightenment ideals, depicts himself as an artist-impresario. Here, front and center, surrounded by examples from his collections and his painter's palette, he lifts a curtain to reveal, for the viewer's delight and instruction, displays of his portraits and collections—his personal museum of the cultural and natural world. Peale directs our attention to the museum as a site of collection and education.

In 1969, Andy Warhol revolutionized established display practices with *Raid the Icebox.* Mining the collections of the Rhode Island School of Art and Design, Warhol as artist/curator chose objects, often-ignored and seen as second-rate, to create a thoroughly unconventional set of installations. In his subversion of convention, Warhol provocatively suggests that the viewer consider the museum as a site of art production. He demonstrates that curating is a creative process and product and that the public space and

An overview of the galleries. Without Sanctuary: Lynching Photography in America *exhibition, September 2001–January 2002. The Andy Warhol Museum. Photo by Richard Stoner.*

[1] Neil Postman, "Museum as Dialogue," *Museum News* 69, no. 5 (1990): 55–58.

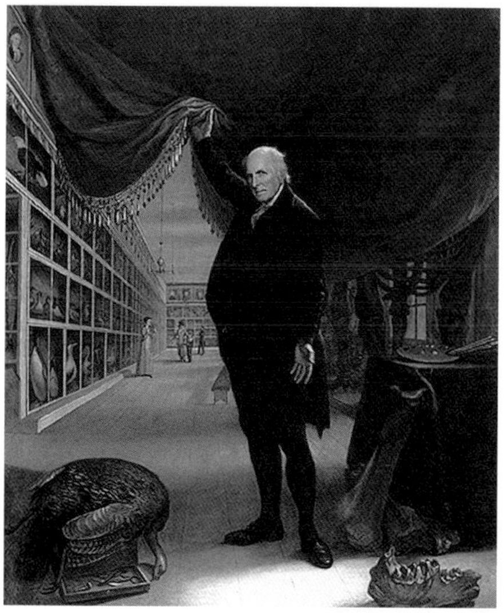

Charles Wilson Peale, The Artist in His Museum, *1822. Oil on Canvas. 103 x 79 7/8 in, [263.5 X 202.9 cm]. Acc no.: 1878.1.2. Courtesy of the Pennsylvania Academy of Fine Arts, Philadelphia. Gift of Mrs. Sarah Harrison (The Joseph Harrison, Jr. Collection).*

collections of the museum can provide the context and materials for artmaking—a sort of satellite of the artist's studio. Warhol's provocative gesture invokes previous avant-garde strategies to underline that art is about the invitation to contemplate and engage rather than a demonstration of craft.

Both Peele and Warhol, although seemingly at opposite ends of the artistic spectrum, point to the immense creative and cultural potential of the museum. Their art offers examples of creative agency from which museums can draw inspiration to craft a new role and practice—the museum as artist.

Museum as artist draws from the rich history and contemporary vitality of museological and artistic practice to engage with contemporary civic life. This way of working involves experimenting with and challenging curatorial and educational practice as well as modes of presentation and display, using the museum's social space and its traditional position as arbiter of taste to focus attention on civic issues. Museum as artist does not suggest that what the museum produces is a work of art; rather, that the museum should be fully engaged in "the *work* of art." As noted in John Dewey's *Art as Experience*, "...the first is physical and potential; the later is active and experienced. It is what the product does, its working."[2] Engaging in "the work of art" is to borrow art's ability to organize and focus energies around life experiences that have significance and value. It is a means of aligning the museum less with the constraints of institutionality and convention and more with the freedom of artistic practice. It is about imbuing the museum with creative agency. It is how we work, our practice. The results are not art products but rather a series of projects that may feature artworks and/or artists developed through a web of creative thinking, dialogue, and exchange. Some are born out of the desire to interpret anew, provoke, or entertain, while others arise from collaborative responses to sociocultural issues and contexts developed with diverse communities and individuals.

Museum as artist is also about breaking free of the conventions that have made the art museum what Theodor Adorno called "family sepulchers for works of art."[3] It is striving to ensure that while respecting artistic intentionality, works of art never simply lie in rest, but are rather embedded in a continual process of (re)interpretation and (re)presentation. Warhol, like many contemporary artists, borrows extensively from museum practices—collecting, documenting, preserving, interpreting. The museum, in turn, can embrace the interdisciplinary thinking, art practices, and narratives of "being an artist" in its approach to programming and display. However problematic it may be to complicate the arena for display or break open "the sepulcher," contemporary times require and provide opportunities for alternative structures, for different visions of how the museum can be in the world, and for new ways of galvanizing creative potential and using social space.

Undoubtedly risky, the notion of the museum as artist is immediately susceptible to cries of relativism. Is this a means of raising the profile of other forms of creative work or redefining the purview of art, artists, and artistic practice? Those who embrace art, through a

[2] John Dewey, *Art as Experience* (New York: Perigee Books, 1934), 162.

[3] Theodor W. Adorno, "Valery Proust Museum," in *Prisms*, trans. Samuel and Shiery Weber (London: Neville Spearman, 1967), 173–186; cited in Douglas Crimp, *On the Museum's Ruins* (Cambridge: MIT Press, 1993), 44.

visual culture approach or a collaborative and/or socially engaged practice may see vitality in challenging the haloing of the solitary genius as the essence of being an artist. Others may see that a separation of church and state, as it were, protects and more properly honors both art and activism. It may seem ironic that The Andy Warhol Museum should present a model of the museum as artist and a collaboratively based, dialogic[4] practice when it was created as a monument to individual artistic genius. Yet, as such, this museum may offer a flexible model of being *both/and*, of embracing tradition and new alternatives, of understanding the mutability of contexts and of not being formulaic in its approach to programming, and of drawing inspiration from artistic practice itself.

[4] I use the term "dialogic" to emphasize a museum's practice, not its programs. This process-oriented understanding of "dialogic" is stressed in Michael Bahktin's theory of the "dialogic" in *The Dialogic Imagination* and John Kuo Wei Tchen's "Creating a Dialogic Museum: The Chinatown History Museum Experiment," in *Museum and Communities: The Politics of Public Culture* (Washington, DC: Smithsonian Institution, 1992).

The mission of The Andy Warhol Museum is to be a vital forum in which diverse audiences of artists, scholars, and the general public are galvanized through creative interaction with the art and life of Andy Warhol. The Warhol is ever-changing, constantly redefining itself in relationship to contemporary life using its unique collections and dynamic interactive programming as tools. Like Warhol, who continually pushed artistic boundaries and practices throughout his career, The Warhol Museum has a history of considerable experimentation with diverse interpretive strategies and display techniques, exhibitions, and programs. Drawing on this experience and its mission to be a "forum," The Warhol recently presented *The Without Sanctuary Project*, one of two projects supported by Animating Democracy. Utilizing historic photographic documentation of lynching throughout the United States as a springboard to address issues of race, bias, and bigotry, *The Without Sanctuary Project* offered The Warhol the opportunity to affirm, build, and reflect on its practice and to explore new ways of working. Subsequently The Warhol presented *Andy Warhol's Electric Chairs: Reflecting on Capital Punishment in America* as a means to explore historical context and present-day views on capital punishment.

Through the lens of these projects this essay explores how museums can creatively operate in the cultural sphere as "civic engager," both within and outside the museum's walls. The essay draws from research, evaluation studies, and reflection to examine what an art museum striving to engage in creative, dialogic, and civic practice looks like: its modes of working; and its challenges, successes, and ongoing questions. Written from both the objectively challenging and advantageously insider position of being an individual fully immersed in The Warhol Museum's life and work, I acknowledge the problematic in the paper's point of view. Yet, it is also, I would argue, a complexity to embrace and to make a case for, with the strong sense that deep engagement in reflective practice from those working within institutions is ultimately, and necessarily, critical to examining practice and to exploring and realizing the possibilities and potential for change.

Museum as artist does not suggest that what the museum produces is a work of art; rather, that the museum should be fully engaged in "the work of art."

THE WITHOUT SANCTUARY PROJECT

As Andy Warhol explored popular media and visual culture in his work, The Warhol Museum sees as one of its roles the examination of the discursive power of images in our lives, whether past or present, art or document. Planned and presented with diverse community organizations and a community advisory committee, *The Without Sanctuary Project*, September 22, 2001, to January 21, 2002, was a multifaceted initiative featuring daily public dialogues, interpretive displays, multiple audience feedback opportunities, artists' projects, and a wide range of programs, at the center of which was the exhibition *Without Sanctuary:*

Lynching Photography in America. Featuring photographs and postcards that document lynching in the United States, these graphic images are laden with the emotional intensity of America's problematic past and present regarding race. Consequently, The Warhol envisioned that the Project would generate community dialogue around race and related issues of bias and bigotry in the context of a local climate fraught with economic disparity and community isolation as evidenced by two high-profile, racially motivated killings, one against whites, the other against African Americans and other minorities that occurred in the summer of 2000. The Project offered an opportunity for The Warhol to contribute to the dialogue on race relations in Pittsburgh and to explore the potential of its mission to be a forum for contemporary issues. In addition to its advisory committee, the institution was also joined by a number of organizations in inviting the community to *The Without Sanctuary Project*—ACLU–Greater Pittsburgh Chapter, African American Chamber of Commerce, Anti-Defamation League, the regional office of the National Association for the Advanced of Colored People (NAACP), The National Conference for Community and Justice (NCCJ), Urban League of Pittsburgh, and the YWCA of Greater Pittsburgh Center for Race Relations.

The Project illustrated how difficult subject matter has the potential to be a galvanizing force for collaboration and dialogue within and across communities and organizations.

In assessing the outcomes of the Project, attendance at *Without Sanctuary* was the highest of any exhibition since The Warhol opened in 1994, with one of the smallest marketing budgets. The rich dialogues, depth of audience response, and community engagement and support attest to the reach of the Project's impact. It also generated significant funding nationally and locally. This response, viewed in the context of the fact that the Project opened 10 days after the World Trade Center attacks on September 11, 2001, demonstrates a collective community willingness to deal with and address challenging and painful subjects. Overall, the Project illustrated how difficult subject matter has the potential to be a galvanizing force for collaboration and dialogue within and across communities and organizations.

The Images: "Unburying" of Place, History, and Identity

The brutal and disturbing images in *Without Sanctuary* initiate a deep "unburying," to use the words of poet Toi Derricotte[5]—an unburying of the legacies of history, place, and identity. Comprising approximately 100 photographic prints and postcards, ranging in date from 1870 to 1960, *Without Sanctuary* documents the history of lynching from Georgia to Illinois. The lynchings are mostly of African-American men, with some of other minorities, women, and children. The images depict hanging bodies and crowds of smiling white onlookers. Some feature terribly burnt corpses, a few show victims just before their death, and several of the postcards reveal pinholes as if they had been hung, trophy-like, in someone's home. In the publication accompanying the exhibition, James Allen, the collector of these images, says of the collection:

> Until I came upon a postcard of a lynching, postcards seemed trivial to me... Studying these photographs has engendered in me a caution of whites, of the majority, of the young, of religion, of the accepted. Perhaps a certain circumspection concerning these things was already in me, but surely not as actively as after the first sight of a brittle postcard of Leo Frank dead in an oak tree. It wasn't the corpse that bewildered me as much as the canine-thin faces of the pack, lingering in the woods, circling after the kill... The photographic art played as significant a role in the ritual as torture or souvenir grabbing—creating a sort of two-dimensional biblical swine,

[5] Toi Derricotte, phone conversation with the poet, September 2001.

a receptacle for a collective sinful self. Lust propelled the commercial reproduction and distribution of the images, facilitating the endless replay of anguish. Even dead, the victims are without sanctuary.[6]

Without Sanctuary exposes untold histories, previously hidden from the mainstream of our historical ephemera. For many white audiences, the "unburying" of the viewing experience is one of encountering a shocking truth and history often unknown or un-emphasized. For many black audiences, and indeed other minority groups, the "unburying" is one of living and reliving traumas of racism and bigotry. For the most part, as James Allen's comment above attests, the "unburying" was not a trauma of violence, but rather of the implied complicity of the crowds of white onlookers to the violence being committed—their smiles conveying comfort in being seen and by extension their affinity with a larger society of bystanders condoning racist mob-rule punishment. Still, why do these historic images "unbury" in such a contemporary sense? Do they derive their power because they are so embedded in a culture that has not fully confronted its past or its legacy? As critic Hal Foster suggests in relation to World War II and the Holocaust, the response is perhaps a symptom of a larger cultural blockage that is a "failure to mourn which in turn prompts a compensatory imperative to remember."[7] Or is it that these images, presenting the stark difference of black and white experience, tap into another failure, one of community and our inability to connect? Is the emotional response a righteousness of release, the relief of oppression finally being seen? Or is it the palpable fear, as we look at this spectacle of spectatorship, prodding our conscience and complicity: what are we not seeing now? Throughout all the stages of *The Without Sanctuary Project*, these and other questions were raised and explored privately and publicly. The "unburying" took many forms.

[6] James Allen, afterword to *Without Sanctuary: Lynching Photography in America*, by James Allen, Hilton Als, Congressman John Lewis, and Leon F. Litwack (Sante Fe: Twin Palms Publishers, 2000), 204–205.

[7] Hal Foster, "This Funeral is for the Wrong Corpse," in *Design and Crime (And Other Diatribes)* (London: Verso, 2002), 130.

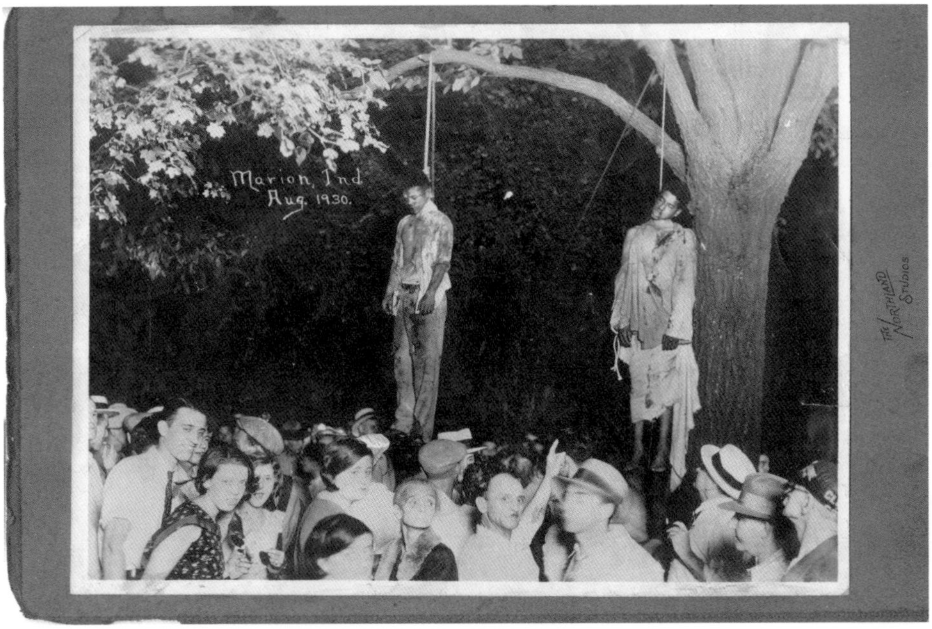

Lynching of Thomas Shipp and Abram Smith, a large gathering of lynchers. August 7, 1930, Marion, Indiana. Courtesy of the Allen-Littlefield Collection.

The Presentation

The exhibition of these images at an art museum raises questions regarding the nature of photography and related media, the relationship between art and documentation, and the aestheticization of imagery of this type. How would the historicity of the lynching images influence their presentation? The art museum experience is traditionally understood as one of an unfettered looking. Would its aestheticizing aura encourage viewers to focus on the images as images and less on the realities of the awful history they revealed? Is it exploitive to present such images for aesthetic contemplation? Any image of war, terror, or torture inevitably, permanently, casts perpetrators and victims in their roles. There is no question that the exhibition of the images, however well-intentioned, (re)presents and uses their pain. Perhaps the only counter-argument is that the only horror worse than looking, is not looking. As avant-garde art practice has demonstrated throughout the last century, there is enormous power in representing images from one context in another context as a way to make us see. It is perhaps the very public nature of collective looking that takes place within an art museum that ensures we truly do look particularly at what seems incongruously in the wrong place.

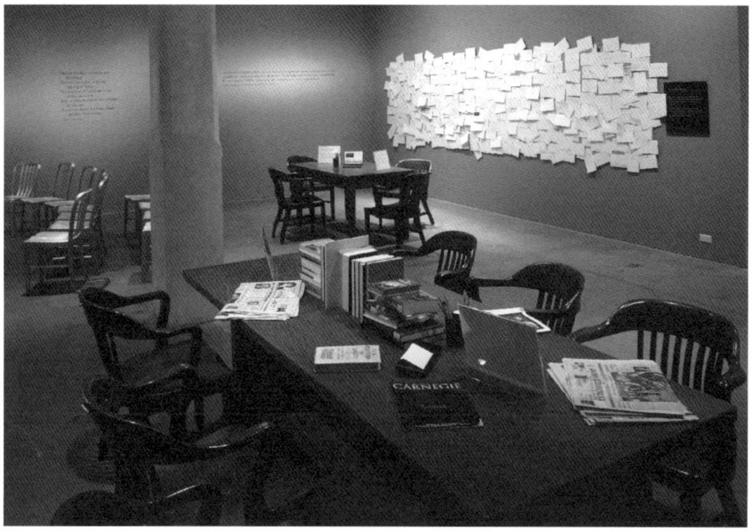

Gallery 602 used as a study and dialogue area for the exhibition. Photo by Richard Stoner.

The issue of the images' presentation at an art museum in general, and at The Warhol in particular, was just one of the many challenges of the enormously complex histories these images unburied. Accordingly, the institution worked closely with a community advisory group and various subcommittees and individuals on the context for presentation. An entire floor was devoted to *The Without Sanctuary Project*. The goal was to display the photographs in an appropriate manner and to provide informative and engaging contexts and spaces that encouraged discussion, contemplation, and reflection. The main gallery featured the photographs, simply framed and chronologically hung on neutral-toned walls. A label identifying the pictured lynching accompanied each image. Opposite this gallery, a 40-foot-long illustrated time line, "African-American Experience, Struggle, and Achievement: 1895–1995," provided a detailed context for the subject of lynching and its history. Developed by historian Liann Tsoukas-Beasley in conjunction with The Warhol, the idea for the timeline arose out of discussion with advisory committee members who stressed the importance of seeing the exhibition framed both in historical and contemporary contexts and in terms of African-American struggle *and* achievement. A revised version was later published, with the Pittsburgh Public School District, in a limited edition for classroom use.

A second gallery featured three displays presenting varying contexts for the exhibition. The role of the artist as activist was explored through the life and work of singer Billie Holiday and her signature song "Strange Fruit," a powerful indictment of lynching. *The Pittsburgh*

Courier and the Anti-Lynching Movement provided important local and historical context through an examination of this seminal African-American newspaper's history and role in the anti-lynching movement. The Warhol worked with Edna B. McKenzie, Ph.D., herself a former veteran reporter for *The Courier,* along with others on the display. A contemporary context was provided by artist Lonnie Graham's collage, "A Contemporary View: Media 1996–2001." The second gallery also featured tables, chairs, comment books, a video comment booth, and monitors that replayed the comments. A small adjacent gallery provided a more private, quiet space. The following are samples of visitor comments:

> I feel sorry for black people because life is very short. And I feel sad because I'm a black person too. And if I were one of them it probaley happen to me to [*sic*]. Age 8.
>
> [This comment was on the opposite page from the above comment, with an arrow pointing to it.] This is what really hurts. I felt this way at 8 too. And now I'm 35. Will things ever change?
>
> January 12, 2002. It took me this long to work up to coming to this exhibit. I still could not look at all the picture. Sometimes hell is right here in the good ol' US of A. God save us all.
>
> When I first read about this exhibit I thought about how no one ever mentioned this in history class, just like the Japanese concentration camps. The ugly, shameful parts of our history are glossed over. As I thought about it, I can recall my elegant little grandmother beginning a story—'And they was going to lynch a niggar'—I'm shamed.

For many white audiences, the "unburying" of the viewing experience is one of encountering a shocking truth and history often unknown or un-emphasized.

The final gallery was devoted to discussion and resources offered by The Warhol, including a wide range of books and other reading materials on lynching and related subjects, as well as information on organizations and activities for "next steps." The walls featured select quotations, including comments from anti-lynching activist Ida B. Wells, Martin Luther King, Jr., artist Adrian Piper, poet Czeslaw Milosz, Eli Wiesel, Margaret Mead, and a visitor who draws a parallel between *Without Sanctuary* and the "lynching" of Matthew Sheppard for being gay. The space provided a large discussion area for the daily *Without Sanctuary* dialogues. Visiting groups were also welcome to use this area. Visitors were also invited to write "A Postcard for Tolerance," a self-addressed, personal resolution that each individual could pin to the wall as part of a collective display. At the end of the Project, The Warhol sent all of the postcards to their respective authors. The goal was to encourage reflection and action on the most personal and individual level and to reinforce the learning experience by reminding visitors of their resolutions weeks or months after their visit. It also was a small way to offer a positive message to counteract that some of the *Without Sanctuary* images had originally been sent as postcards through the U.S. mail. A small sample of the postcards follows:

> Freaks are everywhere! They don't come in any one color. Rely on your instincts and remember this show. Love, Me. (San Diego, CA)
>
> Yo Anth: 1. Read more African-American authors 2. volunteer at the Latino center already. Anth. (Eugene, OR)

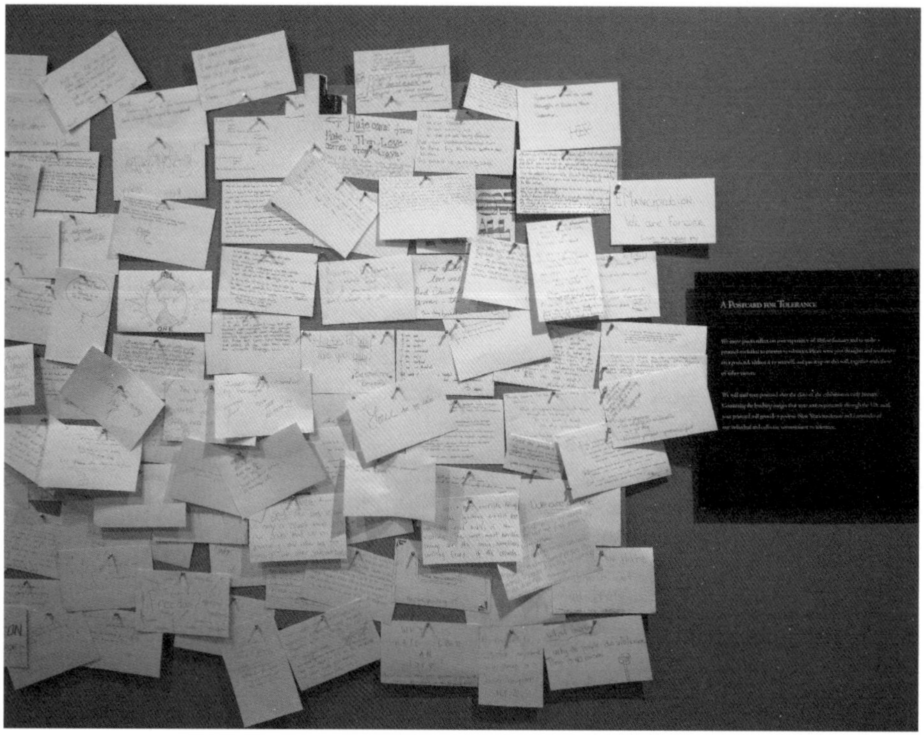

Postcards with messages for tolerance written by visitors to themselves. Without Sanctuary: Lynching Photography in America, *September 2001–January 2002. The Andy Warhol Museum. Photo by Richard Stoner.*

> I am white therefore I'm a racist. From this truth I can move forward in reforming myself. I must be conscious of my privilege, not just today but tomorrow, and the next day, and every day after that. (Pittsburgh, PA)

Public dialogues

> *People really tried to talk. That was miraculous.*
>
> *—Artist/Educator, The Andy Warhol Museum*

Dialogues were held daily (Tuesday–Sunday at 1 p.m. and Fridays at 1 p.m. and 7 p.m). The importance of providing dialogue opportunities was stressed over and over again by our advisory committee. The format offered visitors a structure to share their reactions to the images with other visitors. The dialogues were co-led by The Warhol's artist/educators (practicing artists with experience in education and community-based art practice) and community facilitators from the NAACP, NCCJ, Urban League of Pittsburgh, YWCA Center for Race Relations, as well as other organizations and experienced individuals. The community facilitators were recruited and coordinated by the YWCA Center for Race Relations. A number of planning meetings took place to determine the best way to approach the dialogues with representatives from the organizations listed above. In these meetings, the idea of co-facilitation, the goals and structure of the dialogues, and roles and responsibilities were discussed and determined. The structure of the dialogues was decided to be one of co-facilitation between artist/educator staff at The Warhol and

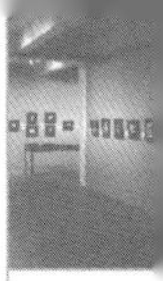

trained volunteers identified by the community groups. The dialogues followed simple steps: the artist/educator and the community volunteer introduced the Project, the role of dialogue, and dialogue ground rules (adapted from YWCA Study Circles and other models); then facilitators encouraged participants to reflect individually by noting their thoughts on blank cards and then to share with a partner; and finally engage in group discussion. The final piece of the dialogue stressed next steps and asked participants to complete a "Postcard for Tolerance" and pointed out available community resources.

Discussion with advisory committee members stressed the importance of seeing the exhibition framed both in historical and contemporary contexts and in terms of African-American struggle **and** ***achievement.***

Approximately 1,000 people engaged in the daily dialogues. Although at times numbers were small for the dialogues, the conversations were always rich and engaging. Another aspect of the dialogue was the wonderful relationships that evolved between the artist/educators and community facilitators, which greatly enhanced the engagement of the community with The Warhol and vice versa. It is interesting to note however that the percentage of participation in the dialogues when compared with overall attendance is quite low (less than five percent). Given how often offering dialogues was stressed by advisory committee members this may suggest that the idea of having dialogues available may have been more important than actual participation in the dialogues themselves. This also made the more informal dialogue opportunities offered in the Project, such as video comment booths, comment books, postcards, etc., extremely important.

School programs

The way we teach history—it's just national myths. We really just tell stories.

—Student Interview

Another point stressed by the advisory committee was the importance of working with the youth audience. School programs featured a two-hour program that included an orientation, viewing of the exhibition, and a dialogue session recommended for grades seven through 12. To assist teachers in preparing for their visits, a teacher resource pack entitled *Art, Activism and Dialogue* was developed. The Warhol also held a teacher open house—which involved lectures, a viewing of the exhibition, and dialogue sessions—and worked in-depth with a number of schools. These included Pittsburgh High School for Creative and Performing Arts (CAPA), one of our partner schools, where students produced a performance and publication, *From Roots to Branches*—a series of student monologues inspired by the images featuring collaboration between visual arts, literary arts, and drama students. The Warhol also worked with other schools suggested by Pittsburgh Public School administrators, as well as several other local and regional public, private, and parochial schools that responded to a request for proposals invitation to participate. Our dialogues and discussions with teachers, parents, and students were rich, surprising, provocative, and revealing. During a dialogue with teachers and parents held in preparation for students' visit to the exhibition, one teacher argued against bringing the students on the grounds that she could teach the unit on tolerance without such images, only to be counteracted by a passionate plea from a parent not to hide the truth from their children. Another dialogue became highly charged when a student from a mostly all-white suburb recognized a relative amongst the white bystanders in one of the images. Overwhelmingly, students expressed frustration at "not being told the truth about history" and a desire to see the subject taught in schools.

Other events

Special events included a wide range of visiting groups such as church groups, diversity coalitions, businesses, groups of college students, and community organizations. Events varied from special viewings of the exhibition and dialogue sessions run by artist/educators, to groups using our dialogue space for meetings and organizing their own dialogue sessions. Throughout the course of the exhibition, several forums were planned. In addition to musical performances and a talk by the collector of the *Without Sanctuary* images, James Allen, the opening day featured forums of scholars and religious leaders. These were the most well-attended and engaged of the forums. Others included an artist forum and one with local respondents. In addition, one of the most successful programs was a poetry reading by two leading African-American poets, Toi Derricotte and Michael Harper.

Creative Practice

> *A person's consciousness is the way in which he or she thrusts into the world. It is not some interiority, some realm of awareness inside the brain. Rather, it must be understood as a reaching out, an intending, a grasping of the appearances of things. Acts of various kinds are involved: perceptual, cognitive, intuitive, emotional and yes—again imaginative... When...a person chooses to view herself or himself in the midst of things, as beginner or learner or explorer, and has the imagination to envisage new things emerging, more and more begins to seem possible. As Emily Dickinson puts it, "The Possible's slow fuse is lit/By the Imagination."* [8]
>
> *—Maxine Greene*

Museum as artist in community

The museum as artist views itself more as an individual, or as Maxine Greene describes, a "beginner or learner or explorer." The museum also adopts a more community-based practice. Particularly appropriate for a single-artist museum, it behaves and functions on a macro level like an artist in community. In adopting a role of artist/creative facilitator/institution, assumed notions of neutrality are qualified with a creative agency. An artist's practice, whose work is strongly rooted in community, can be one that, to use dialogue consultant Patricia Romney's term borrowed from family therapy, is "multipartial,"[9] rather than neutral. However, in addition and in contrast to the analogy of a therapist respecting all sides, the artist distinctly foregrounds, or makes central, his/her practice as one through which others can express themselves. On a macro level, the museum, by aligning itself with an artistic role in its activities and presentations, functions not only as convener, facilitator, or community organizer, but also explicitly and simultaneously foregrounds its creative role as interpreter, provocateur, and catalyst.

Mutability of contexts

Reflecting the more process and performance-oriented practice of some artists, the museum as artist is both a context and a content provider.[10] The work becomes about orchestrating conversations and creating and responding to contexts. The contexts of politics, community leadership, historical and cultural moments, and personal histories and agendas are a creative resource. The investigation of how to structure, utilize, and tap into these contexts to create opportunities for their interaction begins by acknowledging

[8] Maxine Greene, *Releasing the Imagination: Essays on Education, the Arts and Social Change* (San Francisco: Jossey-Bass, 1995).

[9] Pat Romney, comment made at Animating Democracy's *Learning Exchange* (Chicago, IL, November 2001).

[10] Grant Kester, citing the work of British artist Peter Dunn. "Conversation Pieces: Collaboration and Artistic Identity," in *Unlimited Partnerships: Collaborations in Contemporary Art* (Berkeley: University of California Press, 2004).

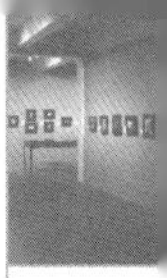

their shifting terrain and recognizing what you do or do not know. For *Without Sanctuary* three key contexts clearly affected the development, presentation, and reception of the Project.

Museum staff struggled with listening and voicing; figuring out how to articulate our point of view and not lose sight of our identity, while being open, responsive, and willing to change those very same points of view.

The Racial Context. The Warhol had already telegraphed itself to the Pittsburgh community as a forum and a risk-taker. This was evident in its programming and its vocal and provocative director, never shy to take a public stance on critical community issues. Nevertheless, leadership and management of the organization are white. The reality of the racial makeup of the organization demanded that *The Without Sanctuary Project*'s evolution and presentation would necessarily involve significant input from the African-American community. The Warhol would need to prove itself before it could be trusted. Certainly, winning an organizational racial justice award a month prior to the opening of the Project was an important honor and a signal to the larger community of its commitment to addressing issues of race. Some in the African-American community knew The Warhol's reputation for quality, and were positively disposed toward collaborating on the Project: "I knew they would do it right." Others who perceived The Warhol as a predominantly white institution, dedicated to a white gay man, were concerned that because Andy Warhol was gay, it would steer the Project to issues of homophobia. As noted earlier, the local Pittsburgh context is fraught with racial disparity, the Project occurred the year after the community was reeling from two racially motivated killing sprees, and many people were keen to explore ways to deal with the problems. Additionally, some African-American leaders voiced concern regarding younger African Americans' lack of knowledge of past racial struggles and disinterest in rallying and fighting for social justice. *The Without Sanctuary Project* was, they felt, an opportunity to teach history and to encourage youth action. All of these motivations, agendas, and concerns influenced the Project.

The Museum Context. Over the course of its brief history, The Warhol had experimented with different forms of programming, interpretive display, and community engagement. Building on a strategic plan conducted in 1999–2000, a new mission statement was written to reflect The Warhol's evolving practice. The timing of *Without Sanctuary* gave The Warhol an opportunity to flex the muscle of this new mission statement and to explore an expanded notion of the museum's potential as a vital "forum" using Warhol's art, life, and practice as a springboard. Significantly, leadership through the museum director fully embraced and supported risk; staff had a desire to learn and take risks and had many of the skills needed to engage and work with community; and of course staff had the expertise required to curate and mount the exhibition and market it.

A National Crisis. *The Without Sanctuary Project* opened 10 days after the terrorist attacks on the World Trade Center. Staff were unsure how this would affect engagement with the Project. A teacher workshop on September 12 was a live-wire of debate. Interestingly, the very vulnerability and emotion people felt post-9/11 seemed to enhance interest in the history, issues, and themes of the Project rather than detract from it. The opening day on September 21 was filled with palpable raw emotion. There was a rousing gospel choir and a series of community speakers, a scholars' panel at which an African-American participant observed that, for the first time "white America feels vulnerable; we've always felt that way," and challenges to the diverse panel of speakers by NCOBRA (National Coalition for Blacks for Reparation). An abandoned car outside The Warhol made us all a little on edge. Interestingly, in "Hidden History: An Exploratory Case Study Looking at the Impact of The Andy Warhol Museum's Without Sanctuary Project," researcher Lynne Conner argues that "while the events of September 11 certainly increased the urgency of the Project's mission, it is likely that the Museum would have accomplished the goal of creating a forum for reasonable (safe) discussion despite it. This is supported by the level of testimony regarding the deep confusion about race and racial politics here in Pittsburgh."[11] Obviously, it is impossible to know what the difference in audience reception might have been without 9/11 but the sheer volume of visitor comments, written and video, and postcards reflecting on the context of 9/11 as well as the numerous mentions in media coverage throughout the exhibition suggest the deep resonance people felt as they drew contemporary parallels with their experience. The Project seems to have provided an important and needed place of reflection at such a difficult time.

[11] Lynne Conner, "Hidden History: An Exploratory Case Study Looking at the Impact of the *Andy Warhol Museum's Without Sanctuary Project,"* (internal report, The Andy Warhol Museum, November 2002), 14.

A new curatorial synthesis

What is critical consciousness at bottom if not an unstoppable predilection for alternatives? [12]

—Edward Said

[12] Edward Said as cited in Hal Foster, *Design and Crime (And Other Diatribes)* (London: Verso, 2002).

A museum engaged in creative, dialogic, and civic practice opens itself up to multiple voices and to creating/curating together with audiences. In the process, the museum plays a critical role in galvanizing energies and promoting a sharing of knowledge that,

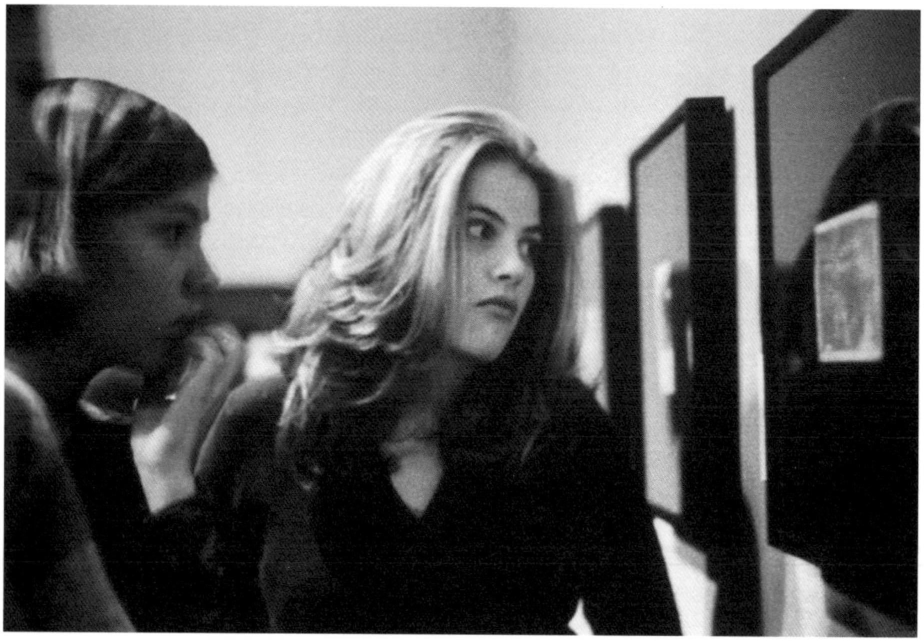

High school students view lynching photographs at the exhibition. Photo by Lyn Johnson.

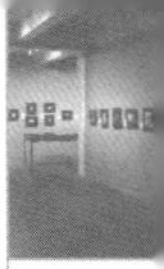

in turn, builds trust and relationships within and across communities. Critical to this practice is that an exhibition or project's development or synthesis—the thoughtful weaving together of research, ideas, conversations, knowledge, and experience—happens together with audiences. This is distinctly different from traditional curatorial practice, where ideas are fully synthesized by an individual curator prior to any public presentation and indeed, sometimes, even prior to internal communication. It is through working together that barriers are broken down and relationships built, as one of our community advisory group members, Malik Bankston, noted.[13] Action is key to relationship-building, particularly important to minority communities that are often highly suspicious of institutional intentions. In the development of *The Without Sanctuary Project*, the contexts for presentation and issues to be considered were discussed and determined in multiple conversations, from informal chats to advisory committee meetings. The synthesis of the Project was mutually constructed. The Warhol brought its curatorial expertise; the committee members and diverse individual collaborators brought their practices and knowledge of community, history, and local contexts.

13 Malik Bankston, conversation with community advisory committee member during *The Without Sanctuary Project*.

Opening the curatorial process up to different forms of synthesis challenges both internal and external perceptions of what art museums do and how they work: curating becomes a function and not necessarily an individual role; a museum's expertise manifests itself as a weaving together of different strands of knowledge, as opposed to being the holder of knowledge; and art's creative processes and historical and cultural contexts are highlighted. The art museum experience becomes less about looking at art, and more about making sense of the world. All of this, of course, questions the art museum as elite institution and as showcase for connoisseurship and artistic genius.

In his essay "Conversation Pieces: Collaboration and Artistic Identity," Grant Kester reflects that an aesthetic of collaboration needs to "evoke instead a form of art practice defined by openness, listening and intersubjective vulnerability."[14] This is hard, and doubly so when dealing with such emotional and volatile subjects as race. *The Without Sanctuary Project*, particularly in its development stages, was marked by what I can only describe as a constant state of rawness and self and institutional-questioning. Museum staff struggled with listening and voicing; figuring out how to articulate our point of view and not lose sight of our identity, while being open, responsive, and willing to change those very same points of view. Each conversation, faux pas, consultation, pointed comment, or attack, over time, built solid foundations for our work, enabling us to speak to the broader community from a position of strength. Although this kind of synthesis is messy, destabilizing, complex, slow, and often frustrating, it is immensely rich, dynamic, and in many ways has more impact in its collective reach and engagement. Contrary to some critics' cry that such practices result in "a legacy of compromise that leads to banality" or "vapid populism,"[15] this way of working does not call upon the museum to eschew its expertise or to simply do what the community wants. Rather, it demands a fuller expression of that expertise interwoven with the contexts of people's lives. The processes of trust, relationship-building, and programmatic experimentation involved in such work sets the stage for future projects where even richer and deeper explorations may be possible. Embracing a new kind of curatorial synthesis or art practice is not about replacing one model for another—such as the narrative of sole artistic genius for one of collaboration. It is about seeing the potential of new narratives of making or curating and finding interesting ways for them to coexist.

14 Grant Kester, ibid.

15 Michael Kimmelman, article on 9/11 memorial, *New York Times*, December 8, 2003.

Dialogic Practice

Museum as public space for private reflection made public

> *To be honest about race demands that one be honest about one's racial attitudes. The fear of revealing these dirty secrets has hindered race talk for decades. The irony is that it is only by revealing such secrets that race talk can be effective. It might make better sense for those officials, teachers, and institutions committed to improving race relations in America to encourage self-inquiry on the most personal, rather than the most public, level.*[16]
>
> *—Maurice Berger*

[16] Maurice Berger, *White Lies: Race and the Myths of Whiteness* (New York: Farrar, Straus and Giroux, 1999), 180.

> *Lucy: Today you were angry because of how unprepared you felt. Angry because you have had 18 years of school and never once were you shown the truth about this country. You were angry because authors and teachers picked and chose what they wanted to include in their histories. You vowed not to let your children feel that way.*[17]
>
> *—Museum Visitor*

[17] Written on the opening day of *The Without Sanctuary Project*, this was the first of the "Postcards for Tolerance" pinned on the wall.

For a museum to be an effective forum for dialogue, it is key to create a safe place to look, to see and be seen, to articulate and to be listened to, to reflect, and to air opinions. Researcher Lynne Conner's case study on *The Without Sanctuary Project* describes this use of The Warhol's space. She notes that several archetypal forms of personal response predominated—the soapbox, the confessional, the pulpit, and the performance space.[18] Throughout the project, The Warhol not only acted as a public space for private reflection but importantly as a space where visitors could make those private reflections public. For example, visitors could participate in one of the facilitated daily discussion groups, write in a comment book, record their video comment, or complete a "Postcard for Tolerance." Significantly, these various activities allowed visitors to make their reflections public to varying degrees, and all comments could be made in the context of and in relation to other points of view. As Conner notes:

[18] Lynne Conner, "Hidden History: An Exploratory Case Study Looking at the Impact of the Andy Warhol Museum's *Without Sanctuary Project*," (internal report, The Andy Warhol Museum, November 2002), 7.

> Perhaps the single most significant way of measuring the impact of *Without Sanctuary* is through the sheer variety of methods and means by which "dialogues" were launched during its run. The term "dialogue" is used here in its literal context, meaning an exchange of ideas and opinions on particular issues. Dialogues are often attempts to reach an agreement or settlement, but they can be a more basic vehicle ("dia" means "through" or "between" in ancient Greek) used to house a debate. A dialogue can be either public or private and can facilitate a diverse range of intentions.[19]

[19] Ibid., 7–8.

Judging by the thousands of written comments (many of which directly responded to other comments), the hundreds of postcards, and the many hours of video comments, visitors truly availed themselves of these opportunities. Indeed, many more people engaged in these more "private" forms of dialogue than in the more "public" daily dialogues. Importantly, those visitors who may not have been comfortable or drawn to comment themselves could engage with others by reading or listening to different points of view, testing their perspective and responses with those of others. This kind of internal dialogue and responsive understanding is possible through the museum taking an active role in encouraging an articulation of the viewing experience, and foregrounding the diverse nature of that experience. Given the low percentage of visitors who participated in organized forms of dialogue, these private and informal opportunities may be the most important kind of "dialogue" to offer.

Image as a table for conversation: specificity and universality

> *By placing individuals at the center as both actors in and observers of history, we can build a historical culture around participation. Individuals, after all, experience, interpret, revisit, reinterpret—in short, they remember and forget. Nations, cultures, and institutions can't, even though politicians and pundits pretend they can. Individuals can discover, recognize, ignore, cross-examine, fear, dream, hope...by comparing their experiences and interpretations with those of others, individuals create empathy that permits them to enter into the experiences of people from other times, places, people from other backgrounds... People develop their empathy toward strangers not as political choices or philosophical abstractions but from intimate contacts with people around them.*[20]
>
> *—David Thelen*

In a paper presented at a panel held by Carnegie Mellon University's Center for Arts in Society on *The Without Sanctuary Project*, Melissa Ragona, a fellow at the center, suggested that the very specificity of photos, depicting a very specific lynch mob, "nullifies our complicity." She argues that it is the more universal image, such as Warhol's images of electric chairs or knives for example, that "inculcate everyone: you, the viewer; as well as the State; the artist; the accused; and the media."[21] The huge response to the lynching images would seem to contradict the argument that specificity nullifies. Rather, it would seem to be the opposite, as multiple visitors commented upon the smiling faces of the "specific" lynch mobs and drew analogies to contemporary contexts and personal experience. Clearly, the images functioned as lightning rods for individual responses. Perhaps because of this, however, it was often difficult to get beyond the specific response of one person or of one community to address universal themes inherent in the images.

One of the obstacles in moving from the specific to the universal was grounded in the fact that the lynching photographs had been hidden from the collective memory. Once defined as an "image bequeathed to posterity,"[22] collective memory implies collective sharing. The photographs are evidence of hidden memories and images, unshared for the most part and unacknowledged in the national consciousness. This shift from obscurity to newfound visibility requires an emotional processing—a collective witnessing and sharing that draws its power from specific experience rather than universal themes. The experience of *The Without Sanctuary Project* enabled an understanding of the importance of providing a public and collective space to initiate this process—one that cannot be prescribed or rushed. At times this proved challenging for The Warhol and the artistic and academic culture within which it is embedded, a culture inclined to move from the emotional to the more intellectual plane and one where a purely emotional response is often viewed as a lower gear from which to shift. Conversely, many of those from African-American communities with whom we worked were suspicious of a nonemotional response, which they regarded as an intellectualization of the images to avoid dealing with racism. African Americans described

[20] Roy Rosenzweig and David Thelen, *The Presence of the Past: Popular Uses of History in American Life* (New York: Columbia University Press, 1998).

[21] Melissa Ragona, "Unmatched Parallels: The Warhol's *Without Sanctuary* Up-Against and Across-the-Hall from Andy" (paper delivered at a panel on *The Without Sanctuary Project*, Carnegie Mellon University, Center for Arts in Society, Pittsburgh, PA, October 2001).

[22] As cited by Conover Hunt in Conover Hunt, *JFK for a New Generation* (Dallas: The Sixth Floor Museum & Southern Methodist University Press, 1996), 17.

being weary of universal themes and attempts to extend their experience to other biases and bigotries. Such extensions were seen as yet another way to bury a history that has not been told, as a refusal to acknowledge racism, and an unwillingness to acknowledge their pain and its emotional residue on an individual and collective level.

[23] Patricia J. Williams, *Seeing a Color-Blind Future: The Paradox of Race* (Reith Lectures) (New York: The Noonday Press, 1997).

[24] bell hooks, *Outlaw Culture: Resisting Representations*, 1994, as cited in Maurice Berger, ibid., 173.

Patricia Williams, in her book, *Seeing a Color Blind Future,* outlines how this kind of universalizing of racial struggles can often be more about avoidance of—rather than dealing with—racial problems. She demonstrates this through an example of the well-intentioned white liberal teachers at her son's nursery school who urged a happy color-doesn't-matter message, prompted by a racial incident that had precisely shown that it did.[23] Why in matters of race, as writer bell hooks suggests in *Outlaw Culture: Resisting Representation*, do "people just lose their rational capacity to know how to approach something?"[24] At times, being white and a woman co-directing this Project was very difficult. Particularly in the early stages, I can certainly attest to moments in meetings of feeling like my knowledge had been hit with a Mack truck. Community members in turn also struggled with the emotional unburying the images instigated.

While it was an undercurrent at some of the advisory committee meetings, the "push and pull" between specificity and universality, emotion and intellect, and one community's oppression and the oppressions of many manifested itself primarily in the discussions over the goals and format of the public dialogues. From the community standpoint, this was prompted by a fear that The Warhol would steer the conversations to address issues of homophobia; they needed clear assurances that the predominant topic of lynching of African Americans would not be wavered from. This was expressed both directly and indirectly with such comments as "Let's not have folks derail the conversation." While fully respecting the enormity of the subject and community perspectives, The Warhol was nevertheless concerned that the community organizations would overly essentialize the discussions.

...the image, artwork, or document is the table for conversation, a gathering place to share and engage dialogue across perspectives and through specificity.

We saw the images as tables for conversation, not as anti-racism workshops. The story of lynching of African Americans was obviously paramount, but it was important that people could bring to the dialogues what they saw in and felt about the images. Not acknowledging or allowing the expression of other sensitivities and oppressions had the potential to alienate and in turn render people less willing to hear the story of racism past and present. Dialogue committee members could support this approach because, as one of the African-American leaders reflected, she embraced the presentation of *Without Sanctuary* at a "white institution" and indeed may not have done so at a "black institution," because she felt the only way to end racism was through building "white allies," and the exhibition at The Warhol provided just such an opportunity. In turn, The Warhol understood the importance of "black allies" in the planning, development, and presentation of *The Without Sanctuary Project.* Critically, as we negotiated obstacles, museum staff and advisory committee members were vested in making it work. This mutuality was fundamental to the Project's success.

Later on, while still being very complimentary of The Warhol, one of the African-American community leaders expressed regret that they did not have the resources to have presented the exhibition themselves. Without a doubt The Warhol Museum had the power of resources to bring to the table. Were we sensitive enough to this as we tried to be

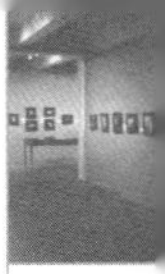

responsive to community concerns? What would have happened had the exhibition been presented at an African-American organization? Did the desire and need to engage "black allies" make The Warhol overlook opportunities to advance the concerns of other established allies, namely the gay community? How much of an issue this was is unclear—internal and external perspectives on this differ—but it is likely that aspects of the Project may have been different with other players at the table.

It may not always be appropriate to strive for balance. Indeed, balance may sometimes be its own bias.

Yes, opportunities were missed, but the challenge of the main subject at hand was overwhelming. I felt and still feel that we pushed as far as we could at that moment or as far as was appropriate given the content. In our approach to the public dialogues as "images as tables for conversation," in our use of quotations in the galleries, in our invitation to diverse community organizations to jointly co-present the Project, and in ensuring inclusive representation at our various public forum programs, I believe that we strove to stress diverse humanitarian themes. It may not always be appropriate to strive for balance. Indeed, balance may sometimes be its own bias. The challenge is to create spaces and opportunities for people to respect one another's struggles and specificity in all phases of a project's planning, development, and presentation. *The Without Sanctuary Project* revealed the importance of honoring and acknowledging the specificity of a community's history and experience, while striving to ensure an openness that respects and does not alienate diverse individual and other communities' "unburying." For the museum as artist and forum, the image, artwork, or document is the table for conversation, a gathering place to share and engage dialogue across perspectives and through specificity. When we gather to talk around an image, we all start from the same place.

Image, context, and response considered equally

Whether or not viewers chose to write in a comment book or participate in a dialogue, it was clear through The Warhol's presentation of accompanying displays and diverse outlets for comments that *image, context, and response* were important and *considered equally.* Interestingly, some criticism from academic circles focused on either the presentation being too "aesthetic" or too "art museum as history museum."[25] Melissa Ragona's comments thoughtfully encapsulate some of the concerns with the latter:

> The Warhol's *Without Sanctuary* show, besides serving as a powerful, graphic indictment of racist America, forces us to rethink the work of Warhol and the voyeuristic pleasure and aversion which his most controversial and often most celebrated works produce. Upon first entering the exhibit, however, it seems we are suddenly cut off from The Warhol Museum and Warhol's work and enter yet another institution, namely the History Museum with its pedagogical accoutrements: historical time-line, rich local contexts, and interactive stations for listening, feedback, and other forms of viewer reflexivity. In a sense, we are taken out of the realm of "controversial art," or the trickster position of Warhol—his provocations of violence: the grisly car accidents, the cool electric chairs, the *Tuna Fish Disasters*, the suicides, and the race riots. Especially, the latter (the race riots)—when viewed up against and in the context of *Without Sanctuary*—take on a forceful historical significance which, with time, has diminished. On the one hand, this is a good thing: it re-invests Warhol's project with a political urgency which has been lost through his iconic presence, his self-portrait, in a sense, as a Campbell Soup Can. But the danger here

[25] Comments at panel discussion on *The Without Sanctuary Project* held by Carnegie Mellon's Center for Arts in Society, October 2001.

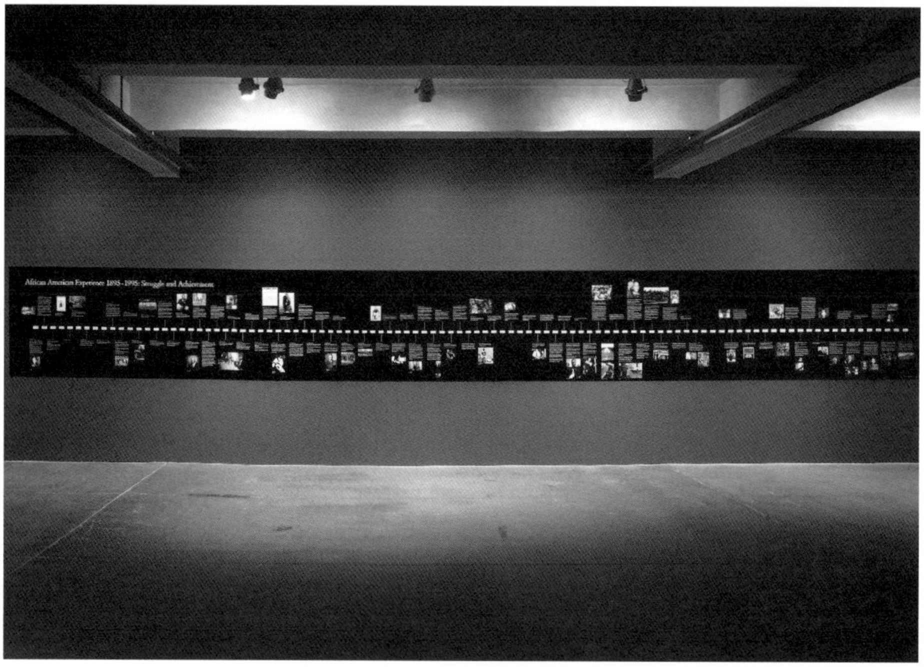

A 40-foot-long illustrated time line, African-American Experience, Struggle, and Achievement: 1895–1995, *provided a context of African American achievements simultaneous with lynching. Photo by Richard Stoner.*

> is a reinscription of an extremely complex Art Project (the power of POP was its seeming simplicity and complicity with the commercial world it attempted to document and transpose) with a historical realism—which seems to be saying, "Look at what really happened." And we do. And in this process, art pales in relation to documentation and explanation.[26]

[26] Melissa Ragona, ibid.

Ragona's comments point to the fact that we have accepted a sort of non-action policy in the art museum environment for fear of overly inscribing the art object, and indeed, particularly when considering contemporary art, the nonart object as art. However, rather than leaving art "open" to multiple interpretations, this privileges the point of view that art speaks without any. I would suggest that it is here where we truly risk art "paling in relation to documentation and explanation." If we are willing to experiment and become more provisional in our approach to interpretation and display, where we mix different strategies—from a very contextual and interactive interpretation to the traditional white-cube presentation—as well as foreground multiple points of view, we signal openness to our audiences and free ourselves from the concern that a particular reading may reduce, overly inscribe, or limit an artwork's potential scope.

In the case of *Without Sanctuary,* as noted by researcher Lynne Conner, the tools and strategies of experiencing art (both art-making and art-consuming) were employed, from encouraging writing and drawing within gallery space to the exhibition design itself, without necessarily engaging the established rhetoric of the art world.[27] This play of combining the aesthetic and the contextual is well illustrated by one of the most successful displays of the project, the large-scale, wall-mural-style time line, "African-American Experience: Struggle and Achievement, 1895–1995" which borrowed from the ritual attention of art

[27] Lynne Conner, ibid, 32.

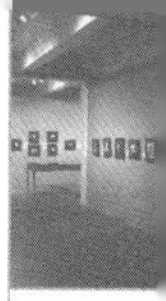

and the pedagogic dimension of documentation and explanation. Placed to directly face the exhibition of the lynching images, the timeline functioned as an informative tool, an anchor for dialogue bracing the pre- and post-viewing experience, and a site of ritual exploration—the walking, pausing, touching, and aura of quiet reverence reminiscent of Maya Lin's "Vietnam Veterans Memorial" in Washington, DC. In essence, it is this liminality, or in-between state, of the art museum as temple and repository of culture and the art museum as forum that produces a powerful place of expression. This, in turn, provides possibilities to reflect on, affect, and create culture.

Framing the initiative as a "Project" brought the public response, and the issues of preparing for it, to the forefront.

A catalyst for discussion beyond the museum's walls

Another important aspect of dialogic practice is that the museum is not only a forum on-site, but also out there in the world through projects that catalyze discussion. Museum staff and community collaborators constantly referred to the many conversations they participated in or overheard with family, friends, and colleagues about *The Without Sanctuary Project*. A popular radio show host featured a discussion of the exhibition on her program. Letters to the editor praised and criticized The Warhol for presenting it, and numerous critical reviews discussed various aspects. All of this shaped visitors' experience prior to coming to the exhibition, engaging a larger community, however tangentially, with the issues. This also raised the awareness level of The Warhol itself. Another vital dimension of dialogic practice was the various outreach and relationship-building initiatives with diverse individuals and groups in the planning and development process. Meetings often lasted hours and were opportunities to open up discussion around personal experiences of racism, to enable trust building, and to correct misperceptions, as well as to talk about and plan for the Project itself. These were fundamental to building the foundations for the Project's success and also prompted the word-of-mouth exchange that was a significant part of the civic dialogue.

"Project" as a way to signal a different and more dialogic practice

At times during the Project, museum staff wondered what would have happened if we had just shown the images without the accompanying "Project" and all its interpretive displays, community dialogues, and initiatives. While it is impossible to predict what the reaction would have been, judging by the multiple and necessary trust-building conversations in the planning process, it is likely that it would have been interpreted as a deliberately sensational gesture, in line with a general public perception of Warhol and The Andy Warhol Museum. It might also have been seen, as director Thomas Sokolowski noted, as an intentionally "take-it-or-leave-it, patriarchal"[28] gesture.

Instead, through *The Without Sanctuary Project*, The Warhol was able to inscribe its mission, and by extension Andy Warhol's work—including its playful elements and avant-garde status—with newfound perceptions of seriousness and responsibility. This also opens up new possibilities for the institution's programming. As Janet Sarbaugh, director of the Heinz Endowments Arts and Culture Program, remarked, "*Without Sanctuary* shows they can take on controversial subjects with sensitivity and without pulling punches. This gives them permission to attempt even more as they continue to explore popular culture."[29]

Another critically important aspect that influenced the context of display and public perception was the presentation of *Without Sanctuary* as a "Project." Framing the

[28] Tom Sokolowski as quoted in Jim Davidson, "Without Sanctuary," *The Magazine of The Heinz Endowments* (Winter 2002).

[29] Janet Sarbaugh, ibid.

initiative as a "Project" brought the public response, and the issues of preparing for it, to the forefront. This in turn led to a greater sense of internal collaboration, including joint leadership from curatorial and education departments, reflecting what researcher Karen Knutson describes in her report on the museum and advisory committee process, as a much more pronounced and importantly cross-departmental "emphasis on visitor experience."[30] The term "project" is of course just semantics. However, from an internal standpoint it nevertheless clearly signaled and valued something more than and in addition to an "exhibition." This was important in suggesting a new way of working, which in turn influenced how The Warhol communicated to the public, from the planning stages to the actual displays.

[30] Karen Knutson, *Report on the Community Advisory Board Process* for *The Without Sanctuary Project*, 10–11.

Performing openness

> *[The constructivist museum] publicly acknowledges its own role in constructing meaning when it displays objects and develops programs. It's important that this human decision-making process—full of compromise, personal views, opinions, prejudices, and well-meaning efforts to provide the best possible material for the public—be opened up to view.*[31]
>
> *—George E. Hein*

[31] George E. Hein, *Learning in the Museum* (New York: Routledge, 1998), 177.

Art history professor Carol Duncan asserts in her book, *Civilizing Rituals: Inside Public Art Museums*, that the meaning of the museum is enacted in its rituals.[32] Like ritual, Duncan's assertion suggests that a museum must constantly (re)perform itself to its publics if it is to put forth an expanded notion of itself and its place in the community. David Carr, professor of information and library science, borrowing from an Umberto Eco essay on improvisational music, "The Poetics of the Open Work," stresses this notion of the museum as a performative space when he suggests that the museum should be an "open work created only in the play of its users."[33] As such, the "open work" underlines the importance of the audience's place within the "work." It also emphasizes a creative and active learning process, since the "work" has to be performed to derive meaning. The museum provides the physical and sociocultural context for interaction, while also itself a creative user, shaping and learning from "the work."

[32] Carol Duncan, *Civilizing Rituals: Inside Public Art Museums* (New York: Routledge, 1995), 2.

[33] Discussed during a presentation at American Association of Museum's *Learning in Museums Seminar*, Chicago, IL, 1995.

How an art museum performs or signals this openness is a subject of much debate. Despite a century filled with artists engaged in institutional critique and significant discussions of curatorial practice, the actual paradigms of display from large-scale international art exhibitions to our seeming *de facto* white wall dioramas, have changed little. Curatorial and architectural language describing exhibitions and new buildings often purports a new ideology of "openness" or "transparency" or the "dictatorship of the viewer" without formats or practices changing in any radical way. It is not enough for a museum to posit itself as "open" with its publics; it must perform it and in ways that those publics recognize.

First and foremost, as *The Without Sanctuary Project* demonstrates, it is critical that this openness is made manifest in the display environment. If we truly want to "open" ourselves up to interpretation, we need to put as much thought into the process of creating an environment conducive to open exchange as we do into how things look; a comment book simply left on a pedestal at the end of an exhibition will duly be treated as such, an afterthought. Secondly, we do not give up our voice, expertise, or role as interpreters. Indeed, opening up demands skill in combining an articulation of our knowledge with listening to many voices, and in explaining ourselves with clarity *and* complexity. Thirdly, when we explicitly acknowledge and open up the museum's mediating role, we need to value that we are learning not only *from* but also *with* our audiences and expect to change in the process. It is in this openness that we become dialogic.

Civic Practice

> *Emotional distance from either objects or audiences diminishes the value and undermines the impact of our work. If we don't care, what's the point?*[34]
>
> *—R. Archibald*

[34] R. Archibald, "Narratives for a New Century," *Museum News* (1988), 33–43, adapted from a speech given at *Building a Sense of Place: A Forum for Museums Partnering with Community* conference, and cited in Karen Knutson, ibid., 15.

Responsibility and using the privilege of the museum's position

Art critic Robert Hughes reflected, in *Shock of the New*: "over the last half-century, the museum has supplanted the Church as the main focus of civic pride in American cities."[35] The idea of civic practice, however, uses the privilege of the museum as civic building to engage with the life of the city as a civic participant. Perhaps the most critical, and, at times, the most overlooked element in the midst of organizations looking for models and formulas of civic engagement, is the importance of intent, of really wanting to. For *The Without Sanctuary Project*, The Warhol's "wanting to" enabled a willingness to make things work and to figure out ways over, around, and through obstacles. It also signaled a commitment to responsive action and to listening that was visibly perceived and valued by those with whom we worked. Creating together, collaborating, and opening up in this way, although very dynamic and rewarding, can at times be extremely frustrating, slow, and fraught with the potential for misunderstanding. It is doubly hard to get into this fray without really *wanting to*. Much of the language around community engagement stresses the importance of accountability and need. Even though this is immensely important, it nevertheless emphasizes a register of imposed "shoulds." As such, figuring out what would intrinsically, as well as extrinsically, motivate museum staff, as professionals and as individuals, to want to work with community is a critical foundational element in the civic engagement process.

[35] Robert Hughes, *Shock of the New* (New York: Knopf, 1981), 391.

***It is doubly hard to get into this fray without really* wanting to.**

It is also important to note that this "wanting" needs to be coupled with responsibility. The museum can boldly tout its civic role and position only if it does so responsibly. Museum as artist is not the unmitigated creative freedom of the lone voice. It is a practice that both benefits from and is burdened by institutionality and is rather a collaboratively orchestrated and owned creativity built through responsiveness to civic issues. In the early stages of the advisory committee process, questions about the rationale of presenting *Without Sanctuary* at The Warhol were often raised. Grant Oliphant, director of communications at The Heinz Endowments, seemed to capture many of the advisory board members' perspectives when he asked: "Why not at The Warhol?" In doing so, he also gave an important caution that the Project should "not be presented in a way that appears at all apologetic."[36] This clear-voiced assertiveness was vital in our communications about the Project, but it was earned over time. Our mission as forum and risk taker gave us our rationale; our engagement with community gave us our confidence.

[36] E-mail correspondence.

Community advisory process

Our community advisory process for *The Without Sanctuary Project* began with engaging an experienced outside local facilitator, Robin Kaye, of Dewey & Kaye Associates. The facilitator's scope of work included helping us to structure our perspectives internally, to clarify our ideas, and to informally consult with community leaders. We knew we wanted and needed to work with diverse community members but were unsure of the best means of approach. This initial process led to the decision to ask the community to help us present the exhibition. The facilitator assisted in setting up a small community advisory planning group to discuss the project and who could and should be included in a larger advisory committee. He then facilitated four advisory committee meetings, while museum staff led several smaller subcommittees. Specific individuals, either independently or on behalf of organizations, worked with museum staff on different aspects of display, dialogue, or programming.

The advisory committee was large, approximately 40 people, all of whom attended the first meeting, while 25 to 30 attended the second and third meetings, and 20 the last. The first meeting was called with a letter of invitation, co-signed by the museum director and board chair. The remaining meetings were called, and ongoing communications facilitated, through a group e-mail distribution. Although there were a few people who attended all the meetings, most just managed to attend one or two. Some members commented that the size discouraged individuals from participating and led them to drop out.[37] Nevertheless, the open-ended nature of the process allowed us to maximize our outreach in a way that was appropriate for this project. The flexibility of the structure and operations of the advisory committee also enabled us to invite people, some of whom were critical of The Warhol's decision to present the Project and others simply interested in participating, to join the committee at various stages of the process.

[37] Karen Knutson, ibid.

Keyworkers and ambassadors

> *When I first heard that The Warhol was bringing this exhibit in, I was the one who said, "who the hell do they think they are?" They heard that, so they asked me to work with them. My director thought it would be good, and they thought it was fantastic… They didn't think they could do it on their own—and this was an asset…*[38]
>
> *—Interview with Race Relations Specialist and Project Collaborator*

[38] Lynne Conner, ibid., 64.

Clearly recognizing what we did and did not know was crucial. It established mutuality between museum and community in a true sense—both needed the other. In this process, key allies were established. It was really only a core group of these allies who thoroughly engaged in every aspect of the Project. For the most part, these were people with professional affiliations to organizations whose explicit purpose was to fight racism and promote tolerance. These allies were essential; they brought their tireless energy and rich knowledge of community to the project, and, importantly, saw the benefit for their own constituencies. They were "keyworkers":

> *…people who can help to open the door between audiences and the museum. Keyworkers may include, among others, youth workers, artists, community workers, craftspeople, adult educators, volunteers, and public employees… They bring*

knowledge, skills, experience, and resources that museums and their staff in general do not have. To differing degrees they also bring their networks, a potentially important means by which access can be achieved and partnerships developed. Keyworkers have influence and responsibilities that are recognized by the target audiences museums seek to reach."[39]

[39] Gabriele Stoger and Annette Stannett, eds., *Museums, Keyworkers and Lifelong Learning: Shared Practice in Five Countries* (Vienna: Buro fur Kulturvermittlung, 2001), 14.

Our keyworkers gave their advice, brainstormed, presented programs, and accessed their own networks for The Warhol. They also promoted and supported the Project, an important part of which involved doing radio and TV interviews together with museum staff. Not everyone, of course, could give this commitment, and another important role was that of ambassador. Here tasks varied, from community participants who volunteered as dialogue co-facilitators, to advisory committee members who simply talked up the Project with colleagues, friends, and associates. All of those involved supported our efforts and worked to convince others of the Project's relevance and importance. Approaching civic practice through stressing individual relationships may have the most impact on perception and engagement. Historian David Thelen makes this point in his book, *The Presence of the Past,* citing Norbert Elias's point that individuals are larger than groups because individuals contain within themselves so many different identities. An individual could be a woman, lawyer, Republican, Chicagoan, lesbian, Irish-American.[40] As such, focusing on working with specific individuals has the potential to access many communities.

[40] David Thelen, ibid., 199.

Valuing different ways of knowing and questioning values

Valuing community experience and seeing things from their point of view is vital in the process of collaboration. This does not mean that the institution gives up control or simply does what the community wants. A key part of the community engagement process is that the museum brings its own viewpoint to the table. This also means getting over the fear of questioning others' opinions and values. Often this means engaging in potentially difficult and emotional issues and conflicts. The difficulty, as Grant Kester notes, reflecting on critical writing around collaborative art practice, is that questioning or criticizing "is often constrained by fear that one will be seen as disparaging the issues or community involved"[41] and as such devalue community concerns and put the actual process of collaboration itself at risk. We need to figure out the obstacles to this kind of honesty, as it is the only way to enhance and build critical discourse around this practice. It is, however, important as museums and their staff wade out into the field of civic engagement that they fully understand and appreciate that if ultimately they are not willing to change and have what they hear influence their practice, it may be better not to go out there at all.

[41] Grant Kester, *Conversation Pieces: Community and Communication in Modern Art.* (Berkeley: University of California Press, 2004).

Communities of practice

It is also important to note that often in museum circles, and art museums in particular, words like "community" can have a somewhat pejorative connotation. Community engagement is at times viewed as a kind of naïve, socially invested earnestness or as dumbing-down and restrictive, or as important but the bailiwick of one individual or department. As noted earlier, the museum is part of the community to be engaged. Here psychologist Jean Lave's notion of "communities of practice" is helpful, where the specific knowledge of any group is socio-culturally constructed. In other words, a community is created through shared practice.[42]

[42] Falk and Dierking, 46–47.

A useful way of conceptualizing community engagement is the museum community of practice engaging with other communities of practice. "Community" in this instance, is not only vested with the overly weighty connotations of politicized minority groups with which the term is often associated in museum and other circles. It is also inclusive of everything from Little League teams and flower groups to cultural theorists. This also underlines the importance of creatively responding to different contexts. Each community may require a different approach. As such, formulaic responses may not work.

Sustainable ways of working

It is fairly standard parlance these days in the realm of community engagement and museums to hear the issues of sustainability and long-term partnerships emphasized as critical. While well-intentioned and driven by a desire to steer away from the kind of tokenistic efforts prevalent in previous decades, it is in many ways a problematic emphasis. The current rhetoric seems to lose sight of the organic way most relationships are built, individual to individual and organization to organization. Indeed, not all partnerships or relationships are, or should be, sustainable. Can you broach collaboration with openness if the goal of sustainability is predetermined? What happens if the relationships within the project do not turn out to be sustainable? Does this then mean we have failed? Often, it is the once-off, specific project that allows people to get to know one another, to work together, and through collective action build trust and relationships, and then to see possibilities for the future. Yet, this project focus would seem to run counter to the current sustainable ethos. We need to shift the emphasis from sustainable partnerships to sustainable ways of working. In this context, museums and communities can embrace working together on once-off projects or long-term initiatives. Some things might prove to be sustainable; most will not. Some relationships may be long lasting and others not. Indeed, some may simply remain as reciprocal resources to be tapped when needed. What is sustainable, or rather, what should be emphasized as key, is the museum creatively responding to and engaging community as part of its practice.

We need to shift the emphasis from sustainable partnerships to sustainable ways of working.

After *Without Sanctuary*

Tangible outcomes and follow-up

An important aspect of the Project was generating tangible, long-term outcomes and follow-up. As a result of many visitor comments, particularly those of educators, The Warhol co-published, together with Pittsburgh Public Schools, a limited number of the time line "African-American Experience: Struggle and Achievement 1895–1995" in a roll-out format for classroom use. The time line was distributed and is being used throughout the Pittsburgh Public School District. In addition, one copy was sent to every public, private, and parochial school in the region. The Urban League of Pittsburgh, as host to the National Urban League conference in Pittsburgh in July 2003, distributed a copy to every Urban League in the nation. This tangible outcome, a product to hold, point to, and be proud of, captured and documented the Project's success for all those involved. It also further solidified an already positive community impression, as well as continuing the Project's goals of reaching out and educating others.

Community arts projects were another form of follow-up. As a means of continuing dialogue within the community and exploring issues raised by dialogue participants, artist/educators

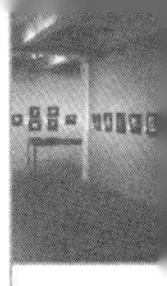

developed small-scale community art projects that brought together art and dialogue. This was an important way not only to continue the dialogue but also to build and further staff competencies and to engage with the issues raised by the Project in a contemporary art context. Four projects were developed: *Free to Be*, an African-American Women's Hair Circle featuring dialogue around the rich touchstone of hair for black women; *Men's Lives*, bringing together black and white men featuring conversations, video interviews, and collaborative large-scale photographic silkscreen printing; *Striking Images*, comprising discussion amongst grandparents who were raising their grandchildren and focusing on the power of personal photographs as a point of departure for exchanging personal histories; and *Scripts for Behavior*, an exploration of the issues facing today's teens featuring dialogues and digitally-manipulated characters to depict scenarios from their lives. An exhibition of these projects was held in the spring of 2003 at Artist Image Resource, a local arts organization with which The Warhol often collaborates.

Assessing impact

> *What I've taken away personally from this experience is enormous. I've simply learned to think about race, something I, as a 22-year-old white woman, had not seriously considered until I began working on the exhibit. Looking at the idea of "white privilege" helped me to find language to facilitate others' experiences as well as my own.*
>
> —*Museum Staff*

> *Their writing in response to the exhibit was some of the strongest they have done.*
>
> —*Teacher Interview*

> *I'm glad I came here today—it was between this & extra sleep on a Sat. morning. This was necessary to see. Being a young, black female living in America is hard & I need to be reminded of how lucky I am that I didn't live through this. I needed to be reminded of how far we've come & how much farther we still have to go. Thank you.*
>
> —*Visitor Comment Book*

> *It wasn't hard to see [the exhibit]. Growing up I was told about lynching all the time. What was hard was knowing that others chose not to see the exhibit. They said it was too hard to see and too hard to talk about it. That was hard for me, to know that people wouldn't force themselves to go.*
>
> —*Student Interview*

...the project galvanized energies and focused a collective attention on racial issues in a manner that was rare for Pittsburgh. Yet, the impact seems to have been mostly felt on an individual level.

There is significant evidence, from visitor comments as well as interviews with visitors and advisory committee members, to suggest a deep and far-reaching impact of *The Without Sanctuary Project*. Research and evaluation studies and conversations with many community leaders attest that the project galvanized energies and focused a collective attention on racial issues in a manner that was rare for Pittsburgh. Yet, it is also true that the impact seems to have been mostly felt on an individual level. For example, attempts made with advisory committee members to bring together political and corporate leadership to discuss citywide issues of racism failed. Informal discussions in communities and some features in the media revealed that many people chose not to attend. How much the Project contributed to racial politics and dialogue in the long-term remains to be determined. What is clear is that the impact will best be manifested by its affect on individuals, the stories they tell, the perceptions they have, and to what degree attendance at *The Without Sanctuary Project* influenced their behavior. The above comments as well as many others gathered through the Project and afterwards reflect a range of responses, personal resonances, and commitments to change. From The Warhol's vantage point, it truly succeeded in its stated goal of providing a vital forum for diverse publics and local communities. The Project generated a tremendous amount of good will toward, and respect for, The Warhol. Considering its mission and the directions for its future programming, this can only reap positive benefits and is now a valued resource. Conversely, many community members now see The Warhol as a resource. Internally, the project generated a sense of playing a truly important purpose in the community. It also built staff competencies and opened the institution up to the possible benefits and enjoyment of working with community on projects in such a direct, museum-wide, and integrated way. One manifestation of this was Youth Invasion 2002, which built on some of the strategies employed in *The Without Sanctuary Project*. Youth Invasion was a multifaceted community engagement program where teens were empowered to take over The Warhol with their "take" on Warhol. The program included displays of youth artwork and youth-curated exhibitions, programs, and publications. Now a highly successful annual program, funded by the National Endowment for the Arts in 2004, the "project" nature of Youth Invasion, its impact on the gallery environment, its development by a teen committee together with museum staff from different departments, and, especially, The Warhol's openness to such a project, was made possible by the lessons learned during *Without Sanctuary*.

...it was our firm belief that it was important to signal to broader publics that The Warhol was not taking sides in the presentation.

It is, however, important to note that the success of *Without Sanctuary* would not have been possible without the considerable foundational experience of past programs and projects, albeit smaller in scale. The Project grew out of an evolving practice, ranging from hosting mayoral debates to experimentation with display and interpretation practices. Subsequent exhibition-based projects have explored themes related to the lynching images: *Andy Warhol's Electric Chairs: Reflecting on Capital Punishment in America*, June 28–November 1, 2003, developed with an advisory committee; and *Inconvenient Evidence: Iraqi Prison Photographs from Abu Ghraib*, September 17–December 5, 2004. Although the scale of the community involvement is less all-encompassing than with *The Without Sanctuary Project*, an ongoing practice of different kinds of community engagement continues, such as an exploration of collective memory through a cross-generational sampling of audio interviews reflecting on the presidency and assassination of John F. Kennedy in conjunction with the exhibition *November 22nd 1963: Image, Memory, Myth*. Material from all these projects is presented online at www.warhol.org. The Warhol is in the process of prototyping various strategies in conjunction with a planned reinstallation and reinterpretation of the permanent collection. Other initiatives are also underway.

ANDY WARHOL'S ELECTRIC CHAIRS: REFLECTING ON CAPITAL PUNISHMENT IN AMERICA

About six months following the success of *Without Sanctuary,* The Warhol was approached by Amnesty International to work with them in relation to their national conference to be held in Pittsburgh, April 4–6, 2003. Initial discussions emphasized the desire to have dialogues and to create sustainable outcomes, in particular to collaborate on the development of educational curriculum and a possible exhibition around the death penalty using Andy Warhol's *Electric Chair* paintings and prints.

Importantly, this project offered an opportunity to apply our "dialogue" knowledge to connect issues of social concern and civic dialogue with powerful examples of Warhol's work. Here, in contrast to the *Without Sanctuary* images, the art is cultural document *and* aesthetic work, raw material *and* symbolic object. Yet, while the lynching images effected a deep "unburying" amongst viewers, how would Warhol's seemingly cool images engender dialogue? Also, *Without Sanctuary* was about exploring unacknowledged historical events that speak to people's contemporary experience in order to teach and learn from the past. All involved would agree that lynching was unconscionable. Capital punishment, however, is very much an issue in the present and one that is highly controversial and polarizing. There are those, including many African-American participants in our *Without Sanctuary* dialogues, who described capital punishment as a "form of contemporary lynching." Others saw it as an appropriate legal and moral sanction for terrible crimes. This project would further explore the museum as forum in concept and practice. If we are to truly embrace the notion of being a "forum," undertaking this endeavor would really challenge us to adopt a multipartial role and to engage diverse perspectives on this issue, particularly when many staff are anti-death penalty, coupled with the wider perception of The Warhol as a left-leaning institution that would be naturally anti-capital punishment. In this case bringing multiple perspectives together would be the most difficult, but arguably the more provocative, course of action.

The Images

> *Warhol's art is charged with incongruity and paradox, he contends that "the less something has to say, the more perfect it is." Despite this preference, his own art has boundless scope, for whatever it has to say; it always says the reverse as well.* [43]
>
> —*Charles F. Stuckey, art critic*

Begun in the 1960s, the *Electric Chair* series is based on a photograph of the electric chair at New York's notorious Sing Sing prison. Warhol used the same image for all his works in this series, only varying the way he cropped it or the background colors he used. The simple image of the empty electric chair, centrally fixed amidst an execution chamber devoid of human presence, is one of the most iconic of Warhol's artworks. How do we read these artworks? Do they, as one critic noted, "offer a home for any set of prejudices the viewer might hold?" Or, do they reflect, as another wrote, "that state of moral and emotional anesthesia which, like it or not, probably tells us...[the] truth about the realities of the modern world?" [44] Did Warhol, as one of his biographers suggests, think that the electric chair simply reflected a "typically American way to go"[45] and as such was as American as Campbell's soup, Marilyn Monroe, and Coca-Cola? Deliberately evasive about his intentions, Warhol's *Electric Chair* paintings and prints are powerful works precisely because they are open to multiple interpretations.

The Presentation

The resulting exhibition, *Andy Warhol's Electric Chairs: Reflecting on Capital Punishment in America,* ran from June 28 through November 1, 2003. It presented Warhol's print series of

43 Charles Stuckey, "Warhol: Backwards and Forwards," *Flash Art 101* (January–February 1981) cited in *The Critical Response to Andy Warhol*, ed. Alan Pratt (London: Greenwood Press, 1997), 140.

44 Steven Kurtz, "Uneasy Flirtations: The Critical Reaction to Warhol's Concepts of Celebrity and Glamour," cited in *The Critical Response to Andy Warhol*, ed. Alan Pratt (London: Greenwood Press, 1997), 254.

45 David Bourdon, *Warhol* (New York: Harry N. Abrams, Inc., 1989), 154.

Electric Chairs, encompassing 10 large-scale prints in diverse colors, double-hung together with several smaller prints and paintings of the same image. Interpretive material was developed in conjunction with various advisory committee members and featured contextual information around capital punishment written by various committee members—from a judge who has presided in death penalty cases to doctoral candidates in history—diverse audio points of view, opportunities for visitors to write their own response to the artwork and the issue, and handmade zines available for visitors to take home. The zines were created by visitors together with The Warhol's artist/educators in the open studio program, The Weekend Factory. They were small booklets with a photographic, silk-screened cover image of an electric chair and consisted of contextual information, questions, points of view, artists' projects, and visitor responses and drawings. The simultaneous preciousness and photocopied/mass-produced feel of the zines reflected Warhol's artistic practice. Five different issues were created during the run of the exhibition. Additional programming included a youth event with performances and dialogues, a panel discussion, and a small number of school group visits, specifically with teachers interested in developing and field-testing curriculum. The exhibition and accompanying programs were presented in collaboration with Amnesty International USA's Human Rights Education Program and Mid-Atlantic Regional Office, the University of Pittsburgh School of Law, Duquesne University School of Law, The Center for Victims of Violent Crime, The Public Conversations Project, and an exhibition community advisory committee.

Many of the same points around creative, dialogic, and civic practice considered in relation to *The Without Sanctuary Project* are true for this project as well. There are, however, some additional distinctions between both projects to note.

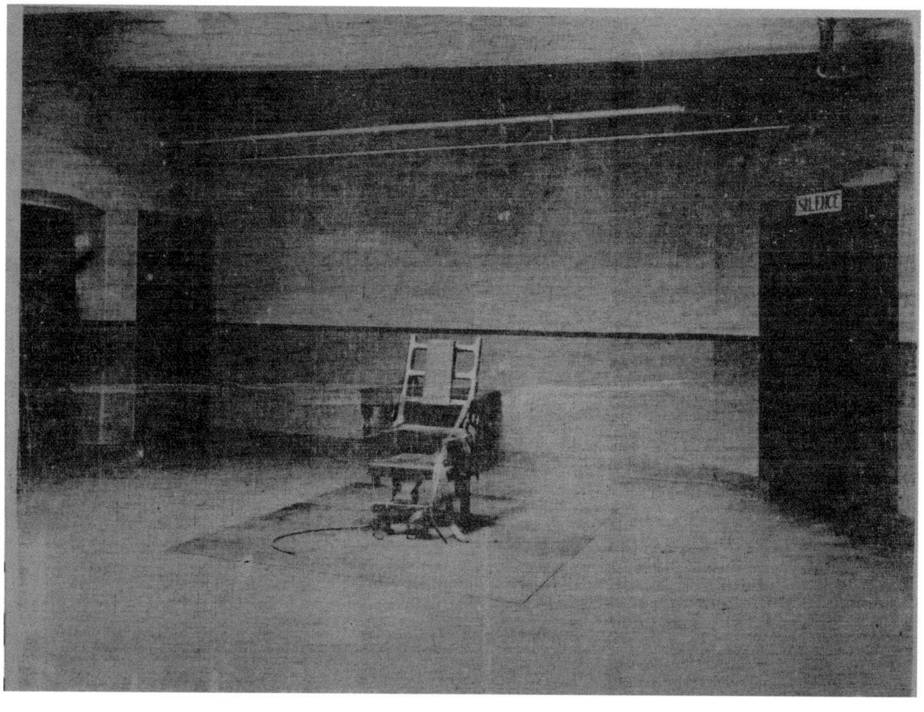

Andy Warhol (American, 1928–1987). Electric Chair, *1964. Founding Collection. The Andy Warhol Museum, Pittsburgh. © 2005 Andy Warhol Foundation for the Visual Arts/ARS, New York.*

Art Museums and Advocacy

One of the key areas where this difference played itself out is our understanding of the role of an institution within the political realm. Is there a place for advocacy? If so, how should that manifest itself? What is the relationship between the museum and advocacy groups? Are they interested in dialogue? In the larger sphere of art and art museums, how are what tend to be left-leaning programmatic practices aligned with what is often right-leaning governance? From the vantage point of programming and dialogue, how do we engage those who perceive a bias or disagree with, more often than not, liberal tenets? Who do we alienate in the process if we do?

Embracing the grey areas and the complexities amidst the polarized positions of pro or con proved at times to be a lonely place.

When Amnesty approached The Warhol, they obviously intended for dialogue initiatives to ultimately support their advocacy ends. It was when the reality of the museum as forum meant sharing the stage with pro-death penalty points of view that their official support of the project came into question and generated considerable internal debate within the organization. As an abolitionist organization that fundamentally believes the death penalty is morally and criminally wrong, the advocacy wing argued that, even though they understood the educational value in the project, acknowledging the other side, and in essence participating with them, gives their views credence and validity. It is as if the death penalty is something debatable. For them there is no pro or con; the death penalty is a violation of human rights. They also felt that, inevitably, arguments against the death penalty get pitted against victims' families' emotions, and in such an emotional realm they cannot argue. From their standpoint, no one would rationally support the death penalty once they knew the facts of an unjust legal system. The human rights education division of Amnesty, however, asserted that from a public education perspective it was important to be engaged in these kinds of discussions. They noted that it is often only as a participant amongst other voices that their advocacy voice can be heard, beyond the choir, to ultimately effect change. The alternative might be no forum at all. This debate happened internally within Amnesty. As the Annual General Meeting (AGM) and possible exhibition/project drew closer, the intensity of the discussions increased. The opposition seemed to take the coordinators with whom I was working by surprise, and they were somewhat overwhelmed and de-energized by the process:

> *The reason people get overly wrought is the timing, a decision has to be made, and it becomes overly dramatic. Since you and I had realized we could not come to any resolution by the time of the AGM there was nothing. The exhibition was there without any interpretive material. The paintings were there, just sitting quietly on the walls, it was a beautiful moment for me; here they were causing all this dialogue, people were going up there and seeing nothing but the artworks, some people were out looking for something evil but they saw nothing. After the AGM there was very little talk afterwards. It was a little dispiriting. It had all this potential that was clearly trumped by getting there.*
>
> *—Phone Conversation with David Yu, Annual General Meeting coordinator, Amnesty International*

From another vantage point, in speaking with different representatives from district attorneys' offices, there was a sense that they become the "whipping boys" for anti-death penalty activists, saying that talking to them is like "talking to a wall." Conversations with police and with researchers working in the field similarly suggested that police officers saw themselves, in a sense, as the last line of order before chaos,[46] totally underappreciated, coping with an overwhelmingly bad rap, and dealing with the realities of crime and justice, while activists functioned in the abstract. At times, some of the pro-death penalty people with whom we spoke, although willing to share their perspectives with us, were less inclined to participate in any formal way with The Warhol or the project. The Warhol approached the Pennsylvania District Attorney's Association (PDAA), which has taken a position in favor of capital punishment, about the possibility, in addition to organizations like Amnesty, of coming on board with official and public support for the project. Following initial discussions with Amnesty, our own internal dialogue, and outside consultation, it was our firm belief that it was important to signal to broader publics that The Warhol was not taking sides in the presentation. Any official support needed to include a range of organizations from different perspectives in order to communicate this openness. The PDAA were extremely concerned about how opposing points of view would be represented. For example, they were interested in ensuring that they knew exactly what statistics Amnesty would present in support of their arguments, so they, in turn, could present counter statistics.

[46] Phone conversation with Ph.D. history candidate Gabriele Gottlieb.

> *The association didn't feel that they would have enough control to prevent this from being anti-death penalty. Control here was a significant aspect… I didn't necessarily agree with the association's position and I strongly suggested that the PDDA be involved in the process. I support the death penalty. I see it as an appropriate sanction. It's the law. If we support capital punishment we should not be afraid of getting the word out about why we support it and we should step up to those challenges. The association, however, did not feel it would be a benefit to sponsor the exhibition. I think they just felt that we would be drowned out by the anti-death penalty voice no matter how it was presented.*
>
> *—Interview with Mathew Mangino, district attorney, Lawrence County, PDDA Capital Punishment Committee*

As we strive toward civic engagement, we are perhaps at our best when we function as a public space for private reflections that are in turn made public.

Both Amnesty and PDAA grappled and dealt with the challenges of what their official and public support of the project meant to their own organizations. In essence, both would have to give up desiring or competing to control the terms of the dialogue. This was extremely difficult for these organizations. One is driven by an abolitionist mission and the other supports the current law for capital punishment and, as such, is less inclined or needing to advocate. One key area of conflict was not in the realm of statistics but rather the emotional register and rhetoric of the language: on the one hand, hellfire and brimstone graphic descriptions of murders, designed to generate visceral response for retribution; and on the other, inventory-like descriptions of a dysfunctional prison system, fraught with errors and fundamentally racist, aimed at appealing to a sense of injustice and an altruistic ideal of a society founded on clemency and understanding. These registers mirror the legal process of prosecution and defense in capital cases, of presenting "aggravating and mitigating" circumstances to decide whether someone should live or die. As such, it appears the courtroom defines the terms of how capital punishment is talked about, which suggests that it may be impossible to ever get to a place of dialogue unless the issue is framed in a radically different manner.

In the midst of waiting for the organizations to decide whether or not they would be able to officially support the project, an important process of letting go took place. Similar to *Without Sanctuary*, the museum as forum became real, both as a physical place and as an idea, out there in the world. Part of this meant embracing the ambiguities and disagreements around presenting these kinds of projects. The process involves shedding the missionary "but we're doing good things" zeal in favor of a sort of caring provocateur role, one that enjoys that things cannot be governed by our intentions. As noted by consultant and meeting facilitator Maggie Herzig, from the Public Conversations Project, a public supporter of the exhibition, there are several different kinds of advocates, and not all of them wish or are able to embrace functioning in a dialogue situation—and may often be best left to their skills of advocacy.[47] Ultimately, PDAA declined and Amnesty gave official support through their Human Rights Education program.

47 Conversation with Maggie Herzig, referencing a Bill Moyers article.

Approximately 40 people were invited to be part of the advisory committee, of which 30 came to the first meeting and 15 to the second. Many members contributed to the audio and/or written points of view and panel texts in the exhibition. Others served on subcommittees for programming and curriculum. However, in contrast to *Without Sanctuary* with its educational history lesson and message of "never again," The Warhol's emphasis on the ambiguity of the artwork and not taking sides meant that advocacy groups and individuals, all potential keyworkers, were perhaps not as able to hang their agenda on the project and were, as a result, less invested. Embracing the grey areas and the complexities amidst the polarized positions of pro or con proved at times to be a lonely place. It is clear, however, from the many visitor comments that people explored the artworks and the issue with great thoughtfulness and the numerous exit evaluation surveys conducted over the summer for the entire museum revealed the exhibition as a definite highlight that "made you think."

Museum as Artist/Interventionist/Researcher

Much of the "dialogue" around this project took place on the phone, "off the record," and internally among the organizations themselves, as they decided whether or not they would offer their public support. How do we capture such dialogue? Is it civic? What roles are art and the museum playing here? How much of this dialogue shaped the ultimate outcome? What impact did it have? As suggested in the context of *Without Sanctuary*, here, similarly, The Warhol seemed to be functioning as an artist in community, in this case employing interventionist strategies. Warhol, his *Electric Chair* series, and The Warhol Museum melded into one idea—provoking discussion, concern, insight, and expression. All of this centered on the various moral, emotional, and sociocultural issues underpinning the capital punishment debate. Most of the conversations always began with a discussion of the artwork; some were familiar with the work, others not. Familiar or not, it was, nevertheless, the table by which we were able to have the conversation. Many of these lasted a long time, where one had the sense that people were working through the issues themselves or using the opportunity for their own dialogue outreach. Others were conference calls with multiple voices and concerns. As representatives of The Warhol, we felt immensely privileged to gradually gain insight into the worlds of those who deal with violent crime, law enforcement, social justice, and advocacy around this issue. All of this informed the development and shaping of the advisory committee and the nature of the exhibition and the accompanying programming.

Being Dialogic and Not Doing "Dialogue"

The most successful dialogue avenues tended to be the more informal approaches. At the beginning of the exhibition, we did try to pull together a formal series of public dialogues by encouraging the advisory committee members to convene small groups to bring to The Warhol for a dialogue. This, however, did not prove to be a successful strategy, as the interest of the committee members was not there and we would not have been able to coordinate this without their enthusiasm. Conversations with some advisory committee members revealed a range of reactions, symptomatic of the fact that "dialogue" can be off-putting for many people. For example, after being asked by the facilitator at our first advisory committee meeting to "listen with resilience," one assistant district attorney good-humoredly gestured to his longtime friend and rival, a criminal defense attorney also at the meeting, saying that he was "incapable of listening with resilience." This amusingly brought to the fore the traditionally adversarial practice of the legal profession which they obviously both enjoy with a certain competitive relish. Busy professionals are often more than willing to bring their expertise to a project, but it is generally more effective when it is task oriented and/or where they see a direct personal benefit—either professional, educational, or entertainment. Their time is limited. For these professionals, there can often be a perception that dialogue is "just sitting around and chatting" and that they "simply do not have time."

> *I think they will be a waste of time and energy unless the conversations are guided by people who have a great deal of knowledge about the death penalty. (Such groups are not necessarily educational; dialogue can easily reproduce ignorance.)*
>
> *—E-mail correspondence with Marcus Rediker, professor of history, University of Pittsburgh, and anti-death penalty activist*

Another undercurrent is that "dialogue" is an emotional process of collective sharing that is fundamentally informed by a psychological/therapeutic model, and therefore, is not informative or educational. We are still very much a culture of authority. Many amongst the educated, professional middle class would much rather sit in a dark room and listen to a lecture than be inveigled to share their reactions. It would be curious to note how many culture or advocacy professionals who plan dialogues would actually participate in such programs themselves. However much of an issue or problem this may be is debatable. It does point to a certain discomfort with the perceived format and connotations of dialogue. This may be informed by a range of possible factors: an anxiety of revelation or loss of authority; cultural paradigms or individual preferences that champion or favor individual over collective opinion; an experience and learning environment that people are not used to or that feels unnatural or too touchy-feely; and a perceived lack of rigor, intellect, or depth in the sharing of opinions. Whatever the discomfort around dialogue, it should not be ignored. As we seek out effective forms of engaging wide-ranging participation, perhaps it is best to shift away from "dialogue" programs per se to ways of being dialogic, from structured approaches to group gatherings, to more interventionist strategies. Using art and/or a museum project as the table around which people can gather for a conversation may be one way of doing this.

CONCLUSIONS

Is all of this civic dialogue? Much of the dialogue generated by these projects was, for the most part, unstructured. Yet, any review of responses suggests that people are clearly dealing with the civic as they grapple with the ideas and issues evoked by the imagery, and with being human and a citizen in contemporary society. Public institutions may play their most significant role in society's civic life by using their public position to encourage self-inquiry at the most personal level. As we strive toward civic engagement, we are perhaps at our best when we function as a public space for private reflections that are in turn made public. To affect this engaged social space we draw on a rich mix of creative, dialogic, and civic practices. The museum as artist embraces multiple new roles—provocateur, catalyst, creative producer, and facilitator—coupled with the traditional ones of educating and researching, documenting, preserving, collecting, and interpreting material culture. It is not *either/or* but rather *both/and*. As an artist, the museum can effect an attitudinal shift, dust off its traditional practices, and be freer to play with how, for whom, and for what we present, display, and create exhibitions and programs. Engaged in civic practice, the museum directs that artistic freedom to "the civic," to the joys and struggles of being human, part of a community, and a citizen in contemporary society. This brings about a marriage of art and public space, a forum to foreground multiple perspectives and reflect life in its complexity. As a dialogic museum, we not only open up our spaces to multiple voices; we also open up how and with whom we interpret to a more dynamic kind of curatorial synthesis as we attempt to make meaning of art and society *together with* our audiences.

Acknowledgement: The author would like to thank Jeanne Pearlman and Terry Smith for their comments and suggestions in reviews of earlier drafts of this essay.

Contributors

Ron Chew has served since 1991 as executive director of Seattle's Wing Luke Asian Museum. Under his leadership, the museum has been an advocate and catalyst for social change in immigrant and underserved communities, broaching complex subjects such as racism, sexism, violence, immigration, exploitation, disenfranchisement, and poverty in Asian Pacific American communities. Ron has guided development of more than 15 award-winning exhibitions and publications at the museum, including the permanent exhibit *Executive Order 9066: 50 Years Before and 50 Years After* and *Reflections of Seattle's Chinese Americans: The First 100 Years.* Ron has been the recipient of numerous awards, including the Washington State Arts Commission Governor's Heritage Award; the Washington Museum Association's Institutional Excellence Award; the Western Museums Association Director's Chair Award; and the Ford Foundation/Advocacy Institute's Leadership for a Changing World Award, which recognizes the work of national leaders in the field of social advocacy and community building. Prior to his work at the museum, Ron served for 10 years as editor of *International Examiner*, an Asian-American newspaper, and for more than 20 years as a community organizer.

Jessica Gogan is assistant director for education and interpretation at The Andy Warhol Museum, where she directs the activities of the education department and other special museum projects. Throughout her career, she has actively focused on building connections between the museum, diverse communities, and contemporary art and culture. In 2001–2002, she was co-director of *The Without Sanctuary Project*. Related civic dialogue projects she directed and co-curated respectively are: *Andy Warhol's Electric Chairs: Reflecting on Capital Punishment in America*, 2003 and *Inconvenient Evidence: Iraqi Prisoner Photographs from Abu Ghraib,* 2004. Other co-curatorial work includes: *Americanisms: Shaping Art and Culture in the 1950s* and *November 22nd 1963: Image, Memory, Myth.* She is currently directing development of an online interdisciplinary curriculum resource using the art, life, and practice of Andy Warhol and co-developing reinstallation/reinterpretation plans for the Museum's permanent collection. Prior to assuming her position at The Warhol she was education officer of contemporary interpretation at the Art Gallery of Ontario in Toronto, Canada and before that at the McMichael Canadian Art Collection in Toronto. Gogan graduated with a bachelor's degree in French and Philosophy from Trinity College Dublin in Ireland, and a master's in Philosophy in Textual and Visual Studies from Trinity College Dublin and Université de Paris 7 in France.

Jeanne Pearlman is the senior program officer for arts, culture, and humanities at The Pittsburgh Foundation. Previously, she served as executive director for Three Rivers Arts, an artist-centered, multidisciplinary visual and performing arts organization that commissions and presents work by regional, national, and international artists in Pittsburgh,

Pennsylvania. Pearlman was the project director for Points of Entry, a multiyear, community-based public art initiative in Pittsburgh, and served as editor for the book that documented the project. She is adjunct faculty at Carnegie Mellon University, where she conducts graduate seminars on critical issues in public art as well as the role of the activist artist in society. Pearlman has written several articles and essays on public art and on German artist Joseph Beuys and his activism in the cause of environmental equity and direct democracy. She is a graduate of the University of Pittsburgh with a master's in the History of Art and Architecture and in Public Policy.

Lynn E. Stern is a New York-based writer and independent consultant with 15 years' experience in the nonprofit sector. She advises philanthropic organizations and nonprofit groups in strategic planning, program design, management, and evaluation. Fluent in Russian, Stern is a specialist in cultural exchange between the U.S., Central and Eastern Europe, and Russia. She served as project specialist to the Ford Foundation's Media, Arts and Culture unit, where she oversaw its capacity-building initiatives in the arts, international creative collaboration, and arts-based civic dialogue, and is serving as consultant to the Foundation's electronic media policy portfolio.

About Americans for the Arts and Animating Democracy

Americans for the Arts is the nation's leading nonprofit organization for advancing the arts in America. With more than 40 years of service, it is dedicated to representing and serving local communities and creating opportunities for every American to participate in and appreciate all forms of the arts.

To learn more about programs, membership, and how you can support Americans for the Arts, call 202.371.2830 or visit www.AmericansForTheArts.org.

Animating Democracy, a program of Americans for the Arts' Institute for Community Development and the Arts, fosters arts and cultural activity that encourages and enhances civic engagement and dialogue. Animating Democracy is a resource for linking the arts and humanities to civic engagement initiatives. Animating Democracy helps to build the capacity of artists and cultural organizations involved in a wide sphere of civic engagement work through programs and services, including:

- A website providing practical and theoretical resources related to the arts as a form and forum for civic engagement and dialogue;
- Referrals of artists and cultural institutions experienced in designing creative civic engagement and dialogue programs on a wide array of contemporary issues;
- Learning exchanges and professional development programs that offer opportunities to learn and share practices and innovative methods in arts-based civic dialogue/ engagement work;
- Technical assistance and consultation for museums, historic sites, and community groups seeking to develop arts- and humanities-based civic engagement initiatives; and
- Publications featuring books, essays, and reports exploring arts- and humanities-based civic engagement.

For more information about Animating Democracy, call 202.371.2830 or visit www.AmericansForTheArts.org/AnimatingDemocracy.

PUBLICATIONS FROM ANIMATING DEMOCRACY

Museums and Civic Dialogue is a publication of Animating Democracy, a program of Americans for the Arts, which seeks to foster civic engagement through arts and culture. Other Animating Democracy publications include:

CIVIC DIALOGUE, ARTS & CULTURE: FINDINGS FROM ANIMATING DEMOCRACY **(2005)**

ART & CIVIC ENGAGEMENT SERIES **(2005)**

Dialogue in Artistic Practice: Case Studies from Animating Democracy

Hair Parties Project, Urban Bush Women

Faith-Based Theater Cycle, Cornerstone Theater Company

An Aesthetic of Inquiry, an Ethos of Dialogue, Liz Lerman Dance Exchange

Cultural Perspectives in Civic Dialogue: Case Studies from Animating Democracy

King Kamehameha Statue Conservation Project, Hawai'i Alliance for Arts Education

African in Maine, Center for Cultural Exchange

Arte es Vida, The Esperanza Peace and Justice Center

Museums and Civic Dialogue: Case Studies from Animating Democracy

Gene(sis):Contemporary Art Explores Human Genomics, Henry Art Gallery

Mirroring Evil: Nazi Imagery/Recent Art, The Jewish Museum

The Without Sanctuary Project, The Andy Warhol Museum

History as Catalyst for Civic Dialogue: Case Studies from Animating Democracy

The Slave Galleries Restoration Project, St. Augustine's Church and the Lower East Side Tenement Museum

Traces of the Trade, Katrina Browne and the Rhode Island Committee for the Humanities

The Without Sanctuary Project, The Andy Warhol Museum

Art, Dialogue, Action, Activism: Case Studies from Animating Democracy

Common Threads Theater Project, Arts Council of Greater Lima

Agents and Assets, Los Angeles Poverty Department

Arte es Vida, The Esperanza Peace and Justice Center

Understanding Neighbors, Out North Contemporary Art House

CRITICAL PERSPECTIVES: WRITINGS ON ART AND CIVIC DIALOGUE **(2005)**

ANIMATING DEMOCRACY: THE ARTISTIC IMAGINATION AS A FORCE IN CIVIC DIALOGUE **(1999)**

To order these publications, visit the Americans for the Arts online bookstore: www.AmericansForTheArts.org/bookstore

Visit the Animating Democracy website for other case studies and writings on art and civic dialogue. www.AmericansForTheArts.org/AnimatingDemocracy.